WHAT EVERY TEACHER SHOULD KNOW ABOUT MAKING ACCOMMODATIONS AND ADAPTATIONS FOR STUDENTS WITH MILD TO MODERATE DISABILITIES

NARI CARTER

Brigham Young University Provo, Utah

MARY ANNE PRATER

Brigham Young University Provo, Utah

TINA T. DYCHES

Brigham Young University Provo, Utah

PEARSON

Upper Saddle River, New Jersey
Columbus, Ohio

Library of Congress Cataloging-in-Publication Data

Carter, Nari.

What every teacher should know about making accommodations and adaptations for students with mild to moderate disabilities/Nari Carter, Mary Anne Prater, Tina T. Dyches.

    p.   cm.

Includes bibliographical references.

ISBN-13:   978-0-205-60836-2

ISBN-10:   0-205-60836-1

1.   Special education teachers—Training of. 2.   Students with disabilities.

I. Prater, Mary Anne. II.   Dyches, Tina Taylor. III.   Title.

    LC3969.45.C365 2008

    371.9—dc22

                                            2008021022

Vice President and Executive Publisher: *Jeffery W. Johnston*

Senior Editor: *Ann Davis*

Director of Marketing: *Quinn Perkson*

Editorial Production Service: *Progressive Publishing Alternatives*

Composition Buyer: *Linda Cox*

Manufacturing Buyer: *Megan Cochran*

Electronic Composition: *Progressive Information Technologies*

This book was set in Bembo by Progressive Information Technologies. It was printed and bound by R.R. Donnelley and Sons. The cover was printed by John P. Pow.

Pearson Education Ltd.
Pearson Education Singapore Pte. Ltd.
Pearson Education Canada, Ltd.
Pearson Education—Japan

Pearson Education Australia Pty. Limited
Pearson Education North Asia Ltd.
Pearson Educación de Mexico. S.A. de C.V.
Pearson Education Malaysia Pte. Ltd.

Merrill
is an imprint of

www.pearsonhighered.com

10 9 8 7 6 5 4 3 2 1
ISBN 13: 978-0-205-60836-2
ISBN 10: 0-205-60836-1

CONTENTS

PART II

Accessing General Education Curriculum   41

PART III

Assessing Learning   81

Tables

Figures

PREFACE

PURPOSE OF THE BOOK

We wrote this book to serve as a guide and resource for general education teachers who teach students with mild to moderate disabilities. The book describes some difficulties students with disabilities experience in school and provides evidence-based teaching suggestions. Many of these suggestions may also benefit students without disabilities, as teachers differentiate instruction to meet the needs of all learners in the classroom.

Differentiated instruction is practiced in many classrooms. When students with disabilities are included in general education classes, however, the law requires teachers to provide individualized supports that enable students to access and make progress in the general education curriculum. Accommodations and adaptations are ways to provide students with needed support. Accommodations and adaptations differ. Accommodations change the manner in which a response is required or the way an assessment is administered, but they do not change the difficulty level of the task. Adaptations alter or modify the level of content difficulty.

More specifically, "accommodations change the input and/or output method used by the teacher and/or the student related to the intended instructional outcome" (King-Sears, 2001, p. 73). For example, students with writing disabilities may be allowed to orally respond or use a scribe, rather than write their responses on a test; or they may be allowed to orally present a project rather than submit it in writing. On the other hand, adaptations allow for the level of difficulty to be altered. For example, if students in a class are required to write definitions of new vocabulary words, an adaptation that reduces the difficulty of the assignment would be to allow a student to match words with definitions rather than writing definitions.

Throughout this book we provide examples of specific classroom accommodations and instructional adaptations that you can implement in your classroom. Of course, before selecting any given suggestion, you need to determine which particular learning problem your student is experiencing; this can be done through targeted instructional assessment. Then you can select the suggestion that most closely addresses the problem your student is having. This book will not answer all of your questions, and you are encouraged to consult with other successful teachers and to access the resources listed in the back.

ORGANIZATION OF THIS BOOK

This book is divided into four major sections. In the first section we discuss common learning problems among students with disabilities and provide suggestions for adapting instruction and making accommodations that address the problems described. In the second section we discuss issues related to accessing general education curriculum as well as options for enabling students to access the curriculum. Section three focuses on assessing student performance and providing accommodations that enable students to demonstrate achievement on classroom and state- and district-wide assessments. And finally, section four is more specific in that we provide suggestions for making content area accommodations and adaptations.

CULTURALLY/LINGUISTICALLY DIVERSE STUDENTS

In addition to providing suggestions for adapting instruction and making accommodations for students with mild to moderate disabilities, we also provide suggestions to teachers who work with students with disabilities from culturally and linguistically diverse (CLD) backgrounds.

Schools are serving increasingly more students with disabilities from diverse backgrounds. Such diversity can be defined across many different dimensions, such as nationality, ethnicity, religion, class, or linguistic origin. Given changing student demographics, we include teaching suggestions for culturally diverse populations under each major section. We focus these suggestions primarily on English Language Learners (ELLs) and those from cultural groups who have communication styles and learning preferences that differ from the majority population. However, the suggestions we provide in this book should be considered supplementary to the larger body of work that addresses educational and social issues for CLD students.

STUDENTS WITH MILD TO MODERATE DISABILITIES

For the purpose of this book, mild to moderate disabilities include the following conditions: learning disabilities (LD), emotional/behavioral disorders (EBD), attention deficit/hyperactivity disorder (ADHD), and mild and moderate intellectual disabilities (ID). Prior to discussing accommodations and adaptations for this population, teachers need a basic understanding of typical characteristics of each of these groups of students.

Learning Disabilities

Learning disabilities (LDs) are the most prevalent disability in children and youth. The term refers to a language disorder that manifests itself in difficulty listening, thinking, speaking, reading, writing, spelling, or doing mathematical calculations. A student does not have a LD if learning problems can be explained by other factors such as socio-economic status, cultural difference, or other disabilities (Individuals with Disabilities Education Act [IDEA], 2004). When students are diagnosed as having a LD, they are identified as having *specific* LD, rather than a general disability in learning. Most individuals with specific LDs are affected in the area of reading, although some have difficulty in writing and mathematics. LDs have also been called *specific learning disability*, *reading disorder (dyslexia)*, *disorder of written expression (dysgraphia)*, and *mathematics disorder (dyscalculia)*.

Currently there are two ways schools qualify students as having a LD. First, students are qualified as having a LD if there is a significant difference between their academic achievement and their intellectual ability. Second, if students receive effective instruction and they fail to make academic progress as expected, they may also qualify as having a LD. The latter is referred to as *response to intervention*, or RTI. School districts determine whether to use both criteria or a single criterion for qualifying students as having a LD.

Emotional/Behavioral Disorders

Emotional/behavioral disorders (EBD) are not as prevalent as LDs. EBDs adversely affect a child's academic performance. To qualify as having an EBD, emotional or behavioral problems must persist over a long period of time, and the problems in school cannot be attributed to other factors (IDEA, 2004). Students with an EBD may (a) demonstrate an inability to build and maintain relationships with peers, (b) exhibit inappropriate behaviors or feelings under normal circumstances (e.g., excessive anxiety, aggression, or fear), (c) experience unhappy or depressed moods, or (d) have a tendency to develop physical symptoms such as stomachaches or headaches associated with personal or school problems (IDEA, 2004).

Attention Deficit/Hyperactivity Disorder

Unlike LDs and EBDs, attention deficit/hyperactivity disorder (ADHD) is not a qualifying category of IDEA 2004. Students with ADHD who do not have an accompanying LD may qualify as having "other health impairment." To determine if a student has ADHD, the student must show a persistent pattern of inattention and/or hyperactivity/impulsivity that is more severe than what is typically observed in other children at comparable levels of development (American Psychiatric Association [APA], 2000). In addition, ADHD symptoms must have been observed before age seven and exhibited in at least two settings (e.g., home and school). Similar to other disabling categories, the condition must have an adverse effect on the student's academic performance. There are three types of ADHD: (1) ADHD, predominantly inattentive; (2) ADHD, predominantly hyperactive and/or impulsive; and (3) ADHD, combined, which is both inattention and hyperactivity/impulsivity. ADHD combined is most common among children and adolescents.

Intellectual Disabilities

Intellectual disabilities (IDs) are not as prevalent as ADHD. Approximately 10 percent of students enrolled in special education are qualified as having an ID (Prater, 2007). IDs are also referred to as *mental retardation, cognitive disability,* and *general learning disability.* This disability is characterized by significant limitations in thinking and reasoning, in social behavior, and in practical, daily living skills (such as communication, self-care, and functional academics). Students with an ID need various types and degrees of support (such as structured environments, communication devices, picture-based schedules, and personal assistants) to enable them to successfully function in society.

PART I

ADDRESSING LEARNING PROBLEMS

Imagine that you are in a crowded lecture hall. The room is too small for the crowd. People are standing against walls and sitting on the floor because there are not enough seats for everyone. When it is time for the lecture to begin, the lecturer steps up to the microphone and begins talking in a quiet monotone voice. You are seated toward the back of the room. It is difficult for you to see the lecturer or the projection of her PowerPoint presentation. During the lecture, you find that it is challenging to focus your attention. People around you are whispering, some of the people who are standing near you leave the room, and you can't always hear what the lecturer is saying. Although you were initially very interested in the lecture topic, you begin to lose interest in the lecture and contemplate leaving early.

For students with disabilities, general education classrooms can sometimes feel like the crowded lecture room. Most students do not experience significant difficulty learning new information in classrooms. However, students with disabilities often struggle in school and experience failure and frustration. School learning environments can be problematic for students with disabilities for a number of reasons. Although each student with a disability is unique, examining the general cognitive characteristics of students with disabilities helps to explain why they encounter challenges acquiring academic skills and why they need instructional accommodations and adaptations to help them learn at school.

Typically, students with mild to moderate disabilities have memory, attention, higher-order thinking, and cognitive processing deficits. It is often difficult for them to remember information, focus their attention on academic tasks, and to think and reason efficiently. Given these deficits, learning concepts and acquiring academic knowledge and skills becomes a challenging endeavor for them, leading to problems with motivation. Students who repeatedly experience failure lose their desire to expend effort to learn.

Learning deficits that impact academic achievement also impact social functioning. Learning takes place in social environments, and the social aspects of learning can be just as problematic for students with disabilities as academic learning. Often, student with disabilities have problems understanding social rules and knowing how to behave appropriately in social situations. Some students may need additional classroom support to help them function socially. Teachers can implement accommodations that match student need and make learning easier for students who struggle academically and socially in school.

Part I of this book is divided into five sections: concept formation, memory, attention, social competence, and motivation. In each section we define the topic, provide information to help you understand your students' unique challenges, identify the issue to be addressed, and suggest ways you can adapt instruction and provide accommodations or adaptations that will help students with disabilities learn. At the end of each section, we also provide suggestions for making accommodations for students with disabilities who are from culturally or linguistically diverse backgrounds.

CONCEPT FORMATION

Concept formation is an important aspect of the school curriculum. In fact, all school learning can be reduced to understanding concepts, acquiring skills, or problem solving (Prater, 1998). "Concepts are clusters of events, dates, names, objects, and places that share defining attributes" (McCleery & Tindal, 1999, p. 8). When children learn a new concept, they need to understand the defining and nondefining characteristics of the concept. Knowing a concept's defining attributes enables students to discriminate examples and nonexamples of a concept. For example, the concept *musical chord*, is defined as three or more musical tones played simultaneously. Single musical tones or tones played sequentially rather than simultaneously do not meet that definition and are, therefore, not chords (Prater, 1998). The ability to detect similarities (three or more tones sounded together) and differences (notes played in sequence) help students categorize information and thus understand new concepts (Hayes & Conway, 2000; McCleery & Tindal, 1999).

Possible Difficulties in Concept Formation

Most children learn concepts through observation and experience. They also learn concepts as others directly teach them about the world around them. For students with disabilities, experience and exposure may not be enough to solidify their conceptual understanding. This may be due in part to language deficits. We use language to label objects and to distinguish similarities and differences. If children lack the language skills necessary for labeling things, then the task of identifying salient features or characteristics becomes even more difficult. For example, Peter may describe the bird he sees as a "thing that moves" instead of something more sophisticated, such as a "yellow flying animal." Peter says "thing" because he cannot remember the label "animal" or "bird," and he lacks the descriptive language necessary for describing specific features or attributes of the "thing that moves," such as "yellow" or "flying."

Language deficits become barriers for learning both concrete and abstract concepts. To learn abstract concepts, students must isolate and describe features or characteristics from examples or illustrations and then generalize that information (Hayes & Conway, 2000). When features are hard to describe or understand, abstract concepts can be difficult for students to learn. To illustrate, suppose that Peter's teacher is explaining the concept of *yellow*. The teacher tells her students that yellow is a bright, happy color, and she shows the class numerous examples of yellow objects. The teacher expects her students to understand that color is a defining feature and to understand what bright and happy mean. But Peter does not understand that color is a defining feature, and he is not certain which colors or objects are bright and happy. He is confused when he sees different objects, and he does not understand that the yellow ball and yellow flower are somehow the same. To him they are completely different: balls are things you play with at recess, and flowers are things that grow in the ground. It is difficult for him to learn the concept of yellow because he cannot perceive that despite the differences between the objects, color (brightness and happiness) is a common feature.

Color is a basic, yet abstract concept for students to learn. As students grow and progress through the school curriculum, they are expected to learn increasingly more abstract concepts (e.g., patriotism and freedom). Concepts are, in fact, a key component of any school curriculum, and thus all students benefit from effective concept instruction. However, given that students with mild to moderate disabilities (a) often fail to learn concepts through experience, (b) demonstrate language difficulties, and (c) have particular difficulties learning abstract concepts, concept instruction for this population is particularly vital (Prater, 2007).

Accommodations and Adaptations that Address Concept Formation Difficulties

Fortunately, there are many things teachers can do to help students who struggle with learning concepts. Adapting instructional methods and incorporating learning strategies (tools or methods for accomplishing a task) in instruction are two general ways to address concept formation difficulties.

Use Explicit Instruction When Teaching New Concepts.   Do not assume students will acquire conceptual knowledge without being explicitly taught. Explicit instruction involves modeling new information, guiding students as they learn the information or concepts, providing opportunities for the students to independently practice the concept, and monitoring students' acquisition of knowledge. Explicit instruction is best delivered when it has been well planned, although lesson plans do not have to be lengthy or complex to be effective. If you plan the structure of the lesson you are likely to deliver explicit instruction effectively. The critical planning steps are as follows: (a) determine what you will teach (the learning objective); (b) use concise, consistent language to teach the concept; (c) model the concept by teaching a process for applying knowledge; (d) guide and monitor students as they learn the concept and practice; (e) incorporate effective questioning techniques and elicit high rates of student response; and (f) monitor student performance while providing error correction and feedback (Prater, 2007). A concept lesson plan is included in Appendix A.

TABLE 1.1   Teaching the Concept of Sharing

TEACHING SEQUENCE	ILLUSTRATION
Concrete	Present role plays and then have students describe how the role plays illustrated sharing. ■ A student is coloring and offers to share his crayons with his friend. ■ The teacher has a pet rabbit and shares the rabbit with her class.
Semiconcrete	Present pictures of the following and have students describe how the pictures illustrate sharing. ■ A father hands the keys to his car to his son. The son drives the car to school. ■ Two girls are outside and it starts to rain. One of the girls opens up her umbrella and shares it with her friend.
Abstract	Provide students with short reading passages and have them discuss how the passages illustrate sharing. ■ Matt has a cat. Matt lets Sam pet his cat. ■ Bud has a ball. He lets Pam play with his ball.

Teach New Concepts Using the Concrete, Semiconcrete, and Abstract Teaching Sequence.
This sequence involves using hands-on experience, pictures, and symbolic representations such as words or numerals. Many concepts can be taught using the concrete, semiconcrete, and abstract instructional sequence (see Tables 1.1 and 1.2). When teaching basic addition facts, use physical objects to demonstrate the operation (e.g., two pencils plus one pencil equals three pencils), then move to tally marks or pictures of objects, and finally to the numerals ($2 + 1 = 3$) only. This sequence is also effective when teaching concepts such as social skills. For example, the social concept *sharing* can be taught by first presenting short role-plays that illustrate sharing, then by using pictures that depict individuals sharing, and finally, with written passages that describe sharing.

Relate New Concepts to Relevant Experiences.   Students are more likely to learn concepts when they can relate what they are learning to their own experiences. Plan lessons that provide concrete learning experiences or allow time during instruction for students to relate what they are learning to their own experiences. "Think-pair-share" is a quick and easy way to engage all students in relating new concepts to their experiences. For example, if during a character development lesson you are teaching the concept of *kindness,* use the think-pair-share strategy by having students individually think of an example of someone being kind to them, placing students in pairs, and then asking them to share their examples with their partner. By providing opportunities for students to relate new concepts to their personal experiences, students make connections that help them better understand new concepts.

Provide Graphic Organizers that Visually Illustrate New Concepts.   Graphic organizers are visual representations of knowledge. Information presented in graphic organizers is

TABLE 1.2   Teaching Probability

TEACHING SEQUENCE	ILLUSTRATION
Concrete	Teach the concept of *probability* by having students toss a coin or take candy out of a jar. ■ Students toss a coin 100 times and record the number of times the coin lands on heads. ■ When given a jar of colored candies, students count the number of red candies and the total number of candies in the jar. Then, they write a fraction that represents the probability that a red candy would be selected if one candy is removed from the jar.
Semiconcrete	Teach students how to draw a probability tree that illustrates possible outcomes for an event. ■ Students draw a probability tree that illustrates the probability that a coin will land on tails for three of three tosses. ■ Students draw a probability tree that illustrates the probability a die will land on a six if thrown twice.
Abstract	Students are given five word problems and instructed to write the probability that a specific event will occur. ■ Students solve the following: If given a jar of marbles that contains ten red, three blue, five yellow, and fifteen white marbles, what is the probability that a white or blue marble will be selected if one marble is removed from the bag? ■ Students solve the following: If a letter of the word *statistics* is selected at random, what is the probability that the letter will be an *s*?

arranged in an associative manner. The following are types of graphic organizers you can use to teach concepts.

- **Hierarchical:** information is arranged by major and minor categories.
- **Concept maps:** a central idea is connected to subcategories and details.
- **Sequential diagrams:** chronological order or a sequence of events is represented.
- **Cyclical diagrams:** a continuous sequence of events is illustrated.
- **Venn diagrams:** similarities and differences are presented with similarities overlapping in each figure.
- **Matrices:** information is organized by categories in rows and columns.

A visual representation of a concept is often easier for students with disabilities to process than large amounts of written or verbal language. Visual representations can include representational pictures (such as drawings or photographs) or lengthy text that has been segmented into manageable parts. See Figures 1.1, 1.2, 1.3, and 1.4 for examples of graphic organizers.

Hierarchical

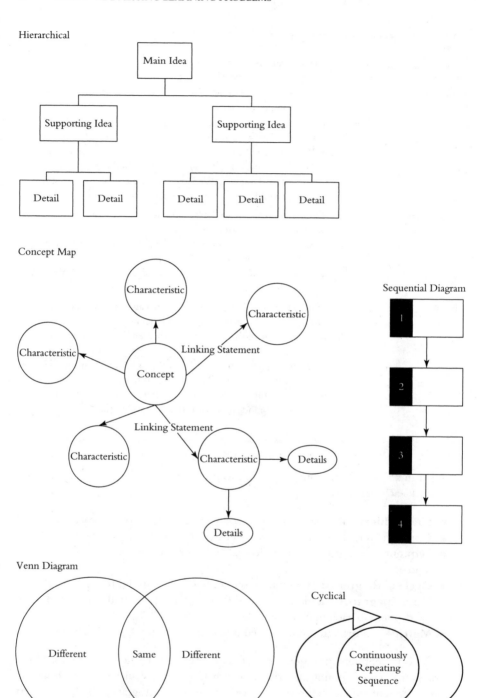

Concept Map

Sequential Diagram

Venn Diagram

Cyclical

Matrix

Category	Category	Category	Category
Example 1	Example 1	Example 1	Example 1
Example 2	Example 2	Example 2	Example 2

FIGURE 1.1   Examples of Graphic Organizers.

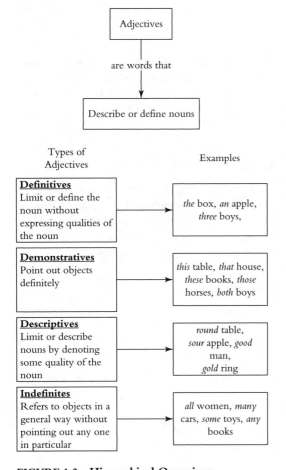

Parts of Speech

Adjectives

are words that

Describe or define nouns

Types of
Adjectives

Examples

Definitives
Limit or define the
noun without
expressing qualities of
the noun

the box, *an* apple,
three boys,

Demonstratives
Point out objects
definitely

this table, *that* house,
these books, *those*
horses, *both* boys

Descriptives
Limit or describe
nouns by denoting
some quality of the
noun

round table,
sour apple, *good*
man,
gold ring

Indefinites
Refers to objects in a
general way without
pointing out any one
in particular

all women, *many*
cars, *some* toys, *any*
books

FIGURE 1.2   Hierarchical Organizer.

TRANSPORTATION COSTS	HOUSEHOLD MAINTENANCE	PERSONAL CARE	FOOD	UTILITIES
Car maintenance and expenses ■ Change oil ■ Gas	Exterior mainte-nance ■ Painting ■ Weatherizing	Clothing ■ Work clothes ■ Casual clothes	Grocery store ■ Food ■ Household items	City expenses ■ Garbage ■ Water
Public transporta-tion ■ Bus fares ■ Light rail tickets	Interior mainte-nance ■ Painting ■ Cleaning carpets ■ Servicing appliances	Grooming ■ Haircuts	Eating out ■ Lunch ■ Dinner	Utility compa-nies ■ Gas ■ Electric

FIGURE 1.3   Matrix Example of Financial Literacy Budget Categories.

Use Concept Anchoring Routines.   Concept anchoring routines are instructional rou-tines for introducing new conceptual information to students and for connecting new concepts with previously learned concepts (Lenz & Schumaker, 1999). The steps of con-cept anchoring routines are described in Table 1.3. A completed example of a concept-anchoring table is included in Appendix B.

Suggestions for Culturally or Linguistically Diverse Students

Teaching concepts to students whose cultural and linguistic backgrounds differ from the dominant culture and language can be particularly challenging. For example, immi-grant children from warm climate countries (e.g., Polynesian Islands) may have diffi-culty understanding vast climate changes, such as winter and snow, until they have experienced them. Similarly, children who live in poverty may not have had the same

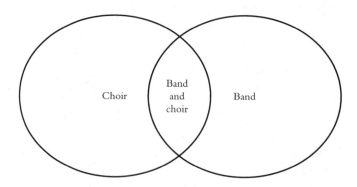

FIGURE 1.4   Venn Diagram.

TABLE 1.3   Concept Anchoring Routine

STEPS OF THE CONCEPT ANCHORING ROUTINE	EXAMPLE
1. State the name of the concept to be learned, define the concept, and tell the students that they will learn the new concept by comparing it with a previously learned concept.	■ New concept: Commensalism is a relationship in which two organisms interact and one is helped and the other is not helped or harmed. ■ Known concept: Lemonade business
2. Ask the students to identify what they know about the known concept.	■ Lemonade business includes lemonade, cups, sugar, space, stand, people, and money.
3. Discuss characteristics of the known concept.	■ Vai needs to locate his stand somewhere and needs the help of his neighbors. ■ A neighbor, Sherri, loans Vai space for his stand. ■ Sherri gets nothing and loses nothing of consequence. ■ Vai is helped.
4. Ask questions to help students see the similarities between the known concept and the concept to be learned.	■ How many living organisms are involved in a lemonade business? ■ How many are necessary for commensalism?
5. Identify shared characteristics and write them on the concept-anchoring table.	■ Two living organisms. ■ One is helped. ■ One is neither helped nor harmed.
6. Ask students to write a statement that summarizes their understanding of the new concept.	*Commensalism is a relationship in which two organisms interact and one is helped and the other is not helped or harmed.*

Source: Lenz & Schumaker, 1999.

experiences as other children, such as traveling or visiting libraries, zoos, or museums. Teachers must be aware of their students' backgrounds in order to bridge gaps between their experiences and the content that is being taught.

Linguistically, words don't often translate directly, which impact students' ability to learn concepts. Teachers need to be mindful of the impact that language and culture play in concept development and must seek assistance from others who are skilled in teaching students from this population, including bilingual or English as a second language (ESL) teachers and others knowledgeable about the culture and/or language of the student.

Use Concept Books to Teach New Concepts.   Concept books are nonfiction books that illustrate and teach new concepts. They are highly visual and usually deal with challenging conceptual vocabulary for English Language Learners (ELLs), such as color, direction, and time (Hadaway, Vardell, & Young, 2004). An example of a bilingual concept book is *The Weather/El Tiempo* written by Gladys Rosa-Mendoza. The book teaches about the four seasons and is part of an English–Spanish foundation series. The text is written in both English and Spanish, and a pronunciation guide for new vocabulary words is included in the back of the book. Another example of a concept book is *Round is a Mooncake: A Book of Shapes,* written by Roseanne Thong. This book teaches about shapes. Many of the objects used to illustrate shapes are of Asian origin. To access children's books written in different languages, visit the International Children's Digital Library at http://www.icdlbooks.org.

Provide Visual Experiences to Explain New English Vocabulary.   Because the English vocabulary of ELLs is so limited, using role plays, actual objects, or visual pictures helps the students to better learn concepts. For example, when teaching the vocabulary word *stubborn*, role play as someone being stubborn, followed by a picture of someone looking stubborn.

Teach Vocabulary Words Necessary for Understanding Concepts.   Linguistically diverse students may not have the English language skills needed to understand concepts being taught in the classroom. It is therefore important to first recognize the vocabulary that might interfere with learning the concept and explicitly teach those English words. For example, when teaching students about making *predictions,* students need to know what *educated* and *guess* means. Teach educated and guess as new vocabulary words. New vocabulary should be explained, illustrated, and used in a variety of meaningful contexts. Students can guess or predict the outcome of a soccer game, what the afternoon weather might be, or how long it will take a seed to sprout after it's been planted. After students understand guess, give them more information (e.g., grass seeds sprout eight to ten days after planting) to help them learn what educated means as it relates to the word guess. Then, students are prepared to learn the concept of prediction. After students understand that making predictions is about making educated guesses, provide students with opportunities to apply their knowledge in ways that relate to their background knowledge and experience.

Teach Students to Use the Visual Content of Textbooks to Understand Concepts.   Many textbooks include diagrams, maps, charts, and tables that illustrate concepts. Students often skip over these chapter elements even though it is important to have them read and to understand this visual material. Specifically, teach students how to read captions, headings, and labels to understand diagrams and charts. When previewing new chapters, make transparencies of visuals and discuss them with the class to provide an overview of the chapter content and concepts (Hadaway et al., 2004).

For Teaching New Concepts, Graphic Organizers in Other Languages are Available.
Graphic organizers in languages other than English can be downloaded from Internet web sites, or you can create organizers written in your students' primary languages (see Figure 1.5). Volunteers, including students' family members, who are bi- or multilingual can assist in making these translations. It is helpful to present these graphic organizers in both English and in the student's native language to facilitate understanding of both languages.

Nombre (Name) _____   Fecha (Date) _____

Causa y Efecto (Cause and Effect)

Evento (Event) _____   Sucede (Happened) _____

Porque (Because)	
Porque (Because)	
Porque (Because)	

FIGURE 1.5   Graphic Organizer in Spanish.

Use Picture-Based Software Programs to Facilitate Conceptual Understanding.   Several software programs exist that are pictorially based. For example, Boardmaker (www. mayer-johnson.com) is a program used for emerging readers and for those who communicate using pictures. The pictures are accompanied with labels in English; however, each picture can be translated into one of several available languages.

If Possible, Provide Textbooks in the Students' Native Language.   Even though some ELLs appear to be fluent in English, conversational and basic vocabulary is different than academic language. In one school, for example, bilingual high school students were consistently having difficulty advancing in math courses in which instruction was given in English. Once they received copies of the math text in Spanish, these students grasped the concepts more quickly and were able to advance to higher math classes.

Incorporate Instructional Conversations in Instruction.   Instructional conversations are extended discussions between teachers and students in areas that have educational value and relevance for the students (Padron, Waxman, & Rivera, 2002). For example, Mrs. Kamalu may use the book *The Three Bears* to teach the concept of comparisons. Rather than having students recite portions of the book (e.g., "The porridge was too hot!"), Mrs. Kamalu has her students make up their own stories using their own examples (e.g., "The porridge was too sticky!"), then engages them in a discussion to promote more complex language use and expression. Use instructional conversations to provide opportunities for ELLs to explore their understanding of new concepts and to use English in an academic setting. The more ELLs hear and speak the language, the quicker they will develop language skills necessary for academic learning.

MEMORY

Memory is the ability to encode, process, and retrieve information. Students use two types of memory when learning new information: long- and short-term memory. Long-term memory involves organizing and permanently storing information for later retrieval. Stored information can be retrieved hours, days, months, and even years following learning. Some long-term memories can even be retrieved over a lifetime. Students use long-term memory and retrieval when they recall math facts, remember how words are spelled, or connect new learning with previously learned information.

Short-term memory is different from long-term memory in that information is remembered for short periods of time, usually from a few seconds up to one minute. Short-term memory is also called working memory and refers to the ability to hold information in one's mind while solving a problem or processing information. We use short-term memory to organize, compare, and code information as it is being processed (Semrud-Clikeman, 2005; Turnbull, Turnbull, Shank, Smith, & Leal, 2002; Zera & Lucian, 2001). Following directions, taking notes, recalling sequences for performing tasks, or comprehending the details of verbal interactions all require short-term memory skills.

Students use both types of memory for almost all academic activities and when interacting socially in the classroom. As students engage in learning activities, they are constantly processing information to be learned, whether it be classroom rules, new vocabulary, concepts, or procedures for solving problems. Learning occurs when information is stored in long-term memory and is retrieved as students apply their knowledge and integrate new knowledge with previously learned information.

Possible Difficulties with Memory

In classrooms, teachers may notice that students with disabilities have difficulty with short- and long-term memory for academic learning and when processing social information (McNamara & Wong, 2003; Semrud-Clikeman, 2005). If a student with a disability has short-term memory problems, the student will experience difficulty in remembering information as it is being processed. For example, when the student needs to copy problems or information from the chalkboard, he or she may not be able to retain the information long enough to copy it. The student will most likely copy one letter or word at a time rather than whole words or phrases—all of which makes copying slow and laborious. In addition, short-term memory deficits may be observed when students are given sequenced instructions such as: "Take out your books, turn to page 32, and begin reading the second paragraph." By the time the student hears the third instruction in the sequence, the student may not remember the first instruction. Teachers may notice that unlike other students, the student with disabilities may not follow the sequence of directions. Understanding students who have problems with their memory will help you to not label them as "lazy," "stubborn," or "willfully inattentive."

Long-term memory can be impacted by short-term memory deficits. When students do not retain information during acquisition stages of learning, it is less likely the information will be stored in long-term memory. Teachers may notice that students with disabilities experience significant difficulty trying to memorize information, and it may appear as though information does not stick—that is, the student knows something one day and then cannot recall it the next. Recalling dates and events, names, ideas, and concepts is particularly difficult for students with long-term memory deficits. Memorizing and recalling math facts and sight words can also be problematic.

Accommodations and Adaptations that Address Memory Difficulties

Instructional accommodations and adaptations that help students with memory deficits are listed below. The accommodations listed involve teaching students memory strategies, providing repeated exposure to material to be learned, and connecting new learning with experience.

Teach Mnemonic Strategies.   When teaching new information, teach students mnemonic strategies for remembering the information. For example, acronyms can help students recall information (HOMES, the five Great Lakes: Huron, Ontario, Michigan, Erie, and Superior). Other mnemonic strategies will be discussed in greater detail in Part II.

Review Previously Taught Information.   When designing instruction for students with disabilities, review is particularly important. Incorporate systematic review and recall activities in instruction to provide opportunities for students to retain and retrieve previously learned information (see Tables 1.4 and 1.5). Reviews should be distributed over time and should be cumulative and varied (Kame'enui & Simmons, 1999).

TABLE 1.4   Planned Review Elementary Example

DATE	ACADEMIC SKILL	REVIEW
Monday	Teach the short *e* sound.	
Tuesday	Teach the *t* sound.	Elementary: Review short *e* sound (say the sound when shown a picture of an object that starts with the *e* sound).
Wednesday		Elementary: Review short *e* and *t* sound (flash card review).
Thursday	Teach the *s* sound.	Elementary: Review short *e* and *t* sounds (sound dictation—students write sounds).

TABLE 1.5   Planned Review Secondary Example

DATE	ACADEMIC SKILL	REVIEW
Monday	Teach map projections, latitude, and longitude.	
Tuesday	Teach compass rose, map legend, and time zones.	Review map projections, latitude, and longitude.
Wednesday	Teach how to calculate time change across time zones.	Review map projections, latitude, longitude, time zones, compass rose, and map legend.
Thursday	Teach scale and the grid system.	Review how to calculate time change.

Use Massed Practice During the Acquisition Stage of Learning.   Students need multiple practice opportunities to acquire skills and knowledge. Massed practice (numerous problems or examples presented in one learning session) provides repetition needed to learn new concepts or procedures. If students without disabilities need three to five practice problems to learn and remember a new concept, students with mild to moderate disabilities might need ten to fifteen practice problems to learn and remember the same concept.

Massed practice can also be drill and rehearsal activities. Drill and rehearsal is practicing a specific skill enough times to master the skill. A piano student might need to practice a passage ten times in a row to master the fingering of the passage, and a young child might need to write the letter "f" twenty times to learn how to form the letter correctly. Research shows that when students drill facts or procedures, they retain learning (Burns, 2004). However, after students have sufficiently learned the new concept, massed practice is no longer appropriate.

Use Distributed Practice in the Maintenance and Generalization Phases of Learning.   Distributed practice enhances retention and allows students to maintain learning (Krug, Davis, & Glover, 1990). When practice is spread out over time, students not only practice the skill but they also practice recalling information. Further, when students are given opportunities to practice using different materials, in different settings, and with different people, they are demonstrating their ability to generalize the newly acquired skills across conditions. For example, after Marionella initially learns to accurately count ten objects (such as counting bears), she practices counting ten objects throughout the week and then counts ten lunch tickets, pencils, and other objects in the classroom and lunchroom. Tables 1.6 and 1.7 are examples of distributed practice.

Provide Authentic Experiences.   When we learn new information, we often connect what we've learned with the learning experience. To enhance memory, provide authentic,

TABLE 1.6 Distributed Practice Elementary Example

PENMANSHIP SKILL	DISTRIBUTED PRACTICE
Lower case *a*	Monday: Introduce *a*. Write *a* twenty times. Tuesday: Review and practice. Write *a* five times.
Lower case *s*	Wednesday: Introduce *s*. Write *s* twenty times. Practice. Write *a* five times. Thursday: Review and practice. Write *s* five times. Write *a* five times. Friday: Practice. Write *s* five times. Write *a* five times.

hands-on opportunities for students to learn and practice new skills. Science vocabulary can be effectively learned through a science experiment, and math skills can be practiced and refined as students work in a school store. Figure 1.6 illustrates how students can learn about rocks with hands-on experience.

TABLE 1.7 Distributed Practice—Geometry

CONCEPT INTRODUCED	DISTRIBUTED PRACTICE
Area of a square	Monday: Introduce area of a square. Ten practice problems.
Area of a rectangle	Tuesday: Review and practice area of a square. Five practice problems. Introduce area of a rectangle. Ten practice problems.
Area of a triangle	Wednesday: Review and practice area of squares and rectangles. Eight practice problems. Introduce area of a triangle. Ten practice problems.
Area of a trapezoid	Thursday: Review and practice area of squares, rectangles, and triangles. Eight practice problems. Introduce area of a trapezoid. Ten practice problems. Friday: Review and practice areas of squares, rectangles, triangles, and trapezoids. Twenty practice problems.

Suggestions for Culturally or Linguistically Diverse Students

In school, students from diverse backgrounds may be learning a new language and participating in a school culture that may be different from the culture in their homes and communities. Because students have to process so much new information, it may be harder for them to remember new material than other students. To make learning and remembering easier, it is important to relate academic content to students' previous experiences, culture, and background. The more connections teachers help students make, the more likely students will remember what is being taught. In addition,

SCIENCE LESSON
Lesson objective: Given a piece of marble, students will write a definition of metamorphic rocks that includes the type of rocks that form metamorphic rocks and the forces that produce metamorphic rocks. *Materials:* Students will be given a small piece of marble obtained from a nearby quarry.

MARBLE	
Definition and Description	
Type of Rock	*metamorphic*
Description	*Color: brown, white, green* *Texture: Smooth*
Definition	*Formed from sedimentary, igneous, or other metamorphic rocks. Heat and pressure change the original rocks into new metamorphic rocks.*

FIGURE 1.6   Science Lesson with Authentic Experience.

culturally and linguistically diverse students may need more repetition and review to remember content taught in a new language.

When Possible, Provide Previews and Reviews in Students' First Languages.   Even though ELLs may be in an English-only classroom, minimally providing previews and reviews in their first language can help students retain information. Table 1.8 illustrates a review in Spanish and in English.

Provide Opportunities for Students to Use New Knowledge and Skills Across Subject Areas and Over Time.   Students are more likely to retain learning when they are provided opportunities to use their knowledge and skills across subject areas and over time (Hoover & Patton, 2005). For example, if students are taught how to write a simple

TABLE 1.8   Spanish and English Vocabulary Review

FARM ANIMALS VOCABULARY REVIEW: SPANISH AND ENGLISH	
Perro	Dog
Vaca	Cow
Pollo	Chicken
Gato	Cat
Cordero	Lamb

sentence with a subject, verb, and prepositional phrase, students should practice writing sentences with this structure during science, health, and language arts. Practice opportunities can be spread across several days or weeks. This instructional tool is valuable for all students, but is particularly vital for ELLs who are learning English with academic content.

Build In-Depth Investigations of Content in Classroom Curriculum.   Study fewer topics rather than a broad range of topics. It is easier for students to understand and retain learning when the subject matter has been thoroughly studied as opposed to given superficial treatment (Zehler, 1994).

Consider the Role of Vocabulary when Teaching Mnemonic Strategies.   Most mnemonic strategies rely heavily on language. In the example provided earlier, when teaching the five Great Lakes, the word HOMES is used. If a student doesn't know that word, the strategy will not help.

ATTENTION

Attention is the ability to focus and maintain thought on specific tasks or activities. As we interact in various environments, we are constantly filtering information and determining how to focus our attention. Usually, the information we process is sensory information—things seen, heard, or felt. When environments provide little sensory input, such as quiet, plain rooms, there are little stimuli to activate or engage our attention. However, if environments are busy with a lot of noise and visual stimuli, filtering information becomes very important because a great deal of information has to be processed before attention can be focused. A student's ability to process and filter incoming stimuli impacts attention span, focusing attention, sustaining attention, the intensity of attention, and sequencing attention (Prater, 2007).

Selecting what to pay attention to is essential for focusing and maintaining attention. This means processing information and filtering out relevant from irrelevant information. In a typical classroom, students are exposed to sound, visual stimuli, and even physical sensations as they participate in instructional activities and interact in social situations. As students hear, see, and feel, they must decide what is relevant and what is not relevant in the current situation—the teacher's voice, the lawn mower outside, or the new pencil sharpener on a friend's desk. When irrelevant information has been identified and filtered out (e.g., the lawn mower and the pencil sharpener), attention can be focused and maintained on what is relevant (e.g., the teacher's voice).

Possible Difficulties with Attention

Most students with mild to moderate disabilities exhibit difficulty with attention. Learning and attention problems are interrelated and usually coexist (Prater, 2007). Students who have attention problems are able to pay attention; however, they find it difficult to consistently maintain and focus their attention. When students with disabilities are interested in an activity or subject, they can successfully focus their attention. Problems with attention become evident when students fail to sustain attention on boring, tedious, or repetitious tasks; are easily distracted by extraneous stimuli; and do not pay attention to details and organization.

Teachers may notice that students with attention deficits often do not follow through on instruction, fail to complete assignments, have difficulty organizing tasks, make careless errors, and turn in messy work. They do not seem to listen when spoken to directly, avoid tasks that require sustained mental effort, and their performance is frequently inconsistent (APA, 2000; National Dissemination Center for Children with Disabilities, 2002).

Accommodations and Adaptations that Address Attention Difficulties

To help students focus and maintain attention, teachers can adapt the classroom environment, incorporate attention strategies in instruction, and teach students how to self-manage attending behaviors.

Review the Day's Schedule.   Students can pay attention better when they know what is expected of them. At the beginning of the school day, briefly review the schedule and post it in an area where all students can refer to it (some students may need individual copies of the schedule to stay on task). Even if classroom routines are established, reviewing the schedule helps students mentally transition from outside activities and prepares them to focus their attention on classroom activities.

State the Learning Objective at the Beginning of Lessons.   At the beginning of a new lesson, state what you expect students to learn from the lesson or solicit the learning outcome from the students. For example, if the lesson objective is to teach students how to write a resume for a job application, introduce the topic of writing a resume and ask a question that prompts the students to state the lesson objective: "What will you learn to do today?" (U.S. Department of Education, Office of Special Education Programs [OSERS], 2004). Then, ask another question that solicits the rationale for learning the skill: "Why is it important for you to know how to write a resume?"

Provide a Written Outline or Graphic Organizer of the Lesson.   Because students with disabilities have difficulty paying attention and recalling previously learned information, a written outline or a graphic organizer of a lesson becomes a visual and permanent reminder of what the student will be learning and what he or she will be required to do during the lesson. It also serves as a homework prompt. When taken home, it communicates your expectations to the parents of your students.

When Introducing New Information, Explicitly Identify Important and Relevant Information.   Because students often have difficulty discriminating between relevant

INCLUDE THE FOLLOWING IN COVER LETTERS:
1. Your name and address. 2. The date. 3. The company's name and address. 4. The subject line. 5. The salutation. 6. An explanation of why you are applying for the job. 7. The closing. 8. Your name and signature.

FIGURE 1.7   Example of Identifying Important Information.

and irrelevant information, telling them directly can help them learn without frustration. Use simple, concise language to tell students what is important. This refers to the content to be learned as well as expectations of the students. For example, when using class discussion to cover a course topic, tell students what they will be held accountable for knowing on the test or for completing a project (e.g., discuss three causes of the Civil War). Or, when teaching students how to write a cover letter, explicitly state what the students need to know: "Cover letters include your name and address, the date, the company's name and address, a subject line, a salutation, an explanation of why you are applying for the job, the closing, and your name and signature." This information can be presented verbally and/or the same information can be given to the students as a handout (see Figure 1.7).

Simplify Directions.   Students are more likely to comply with directions if they are simple and easy to understand. Eliminate unnecessary explanations and use clear, concise language when giving directions (see Table 1.9). In addition, provide simplified directions in writing where possible, so students can refer back to them rather than repeatedly asking classmates or the teacher.

TABLE 1.9   Comparison of Ambiguous and Clear Directions

DIRECTIONS	EXAMPLES
Ambiguous Directions	"Everyone needs to show respect for other people. In showing respect, it's important to understand that people have personal space. Please respect your neighbor's personal space."
Clear Directions	**"Keep your hands and feet to yourself."**
Ambiguous Directions	"I would like everyone to look like they are ready to pay attention to instruction."
Clear Directions	**"Keep your pant pockets on the floor and your eyes on me."**

Give One Direction at a Time.   If too many directions are given at once, students with attention difficulties may become lost or confused. When giving directions to the class, state one direction at a time, wait for compliance, and then continue to give subsequent directions (OSERS, 2004; Salend, Elhoweris, & van Garderen, 2003). For example, rather than saying, "Go to the back table and get your health packet out of the box, get out your health book, turn to page 108, read the page, then take out the purple sheet from your packet and begin working on the assignment," give one direction at a time. Ask small groups of students to go to the back table to get their packets. After the whole class is seated, ask the students to take out their health books. After students have taken their books out of their desks, tell them to turn to page 108. When everyone has turned to page 108, then give the direction to read the material on the page. The directions for completing the work on the purple sheet should be given after the students have read page 108.

Provide Follow-Up Directions.   Sometimes it may be necessary to provide follow-up directions for students with disabilities. Follow-up directions are simplified, clear directions given to students who may not understand the directions given to the entire class. Follow-up directions can be given orally or in writing. After giving the class instructions for starting a grammar assignment, check with the students with disabilities to make sure they understand the directions. If students are unclear about what to do, give step-by-step instructions and monitor their work as each instruction is given. Or, give students written directions (see Figure 1.8).

Use Focusing Strategies such as Study Guides and Advance Organizers to Emphasize Relevant Information.   For new lessons or units, create study guides or advance organizers that direct students' attention to important concepts and information. Most textbooks contain more information than students can reasonably remember or process. Study guides and advance organizers are great tools for highlighting essential information. They can be used to identify vocabulary and concepts students need to learn (see Figure 1.9).

COMMA LESSON

The Teacher's Learning Objective.
When given 10 sentences with lists of three or more items in each sentence, students will rewrite the sentences inserting commas after each item in the list with 100 percent accuracy for comma placement.

The Student's Directions for Comma Placement.
1. Read the sentence.
2. Circle the list of items.
3. Write a comma after each item.
4. Rewrite each sentence inserting commas.

FIGURE 1.8   Comma Lesson.

Unit 3—Rocks, Minerals, and Soil

Rocks

Objective: Students will write definitions for igneous, sedimentary, and meta-morphic rocks and will explain how these rocks are formed.

1. Igneous
    a. Created from:
    b. Formed by:
    c. Texture:
2. Sedimentary
    a. Created from:
    b. Formed by:
    c. Texture:
3. Metamorphic
    a. Created from:
    b. Formed by:
    c. Texture:

FIGURE 1.9   Example of a Study Guide.

Make Assistive Technology Accessible to Students.   Students with attention deficits may experience difficulty processing verbal instructions and may benefit from using assistive technology that helps them to visualize instructions and concepts. Various computer programs are available that help students acquire and use academic skills. For example, Draft: Builder (www.donjohnston.com) is a computer program that guides students through the writing process. When using the program, students create out-lines and map ideas for essays as part of the prewriting process. Then, they combine their outlines with notes to create a written draft of a paper. When the draft is com-plete, students export their documents to a word processing program for final review and printing.

Use Visual Aids to Enhance Instruction.   Students are more likely to attend when visual aids are used during instruction. Use visual aids such as videos, overheads, pic-tures, and graphs during lessons to gain and maintain students' attention.

Frequently Check for Understanding.   Although students may appear as though they understand classroom instruction and are paying attention, ask questions frequently to assess if students are paying attention and comprehending instruction. Requiring stu-dents to respond helps them pay attention, particularly when they don't know when they will be called on. If some students freeze up when randomly called on, privately arrange a cue, such as standing in front of their desk, before you call on them. Or, use shared responses by pairing students. When calling on students during a lesson, avoid pointing out attention differences between students with disabilities and the rest of the class.

Modify the Pace of Instruction.   If the pace is too fast or too slow, students may be lost or bored, and thus may not attend. Teach at a pace that keeps students actively engaged in learning activities. Students are more likely to keep their attention focused when they are busy learning. Your instructional pace is probably too slow if your students look bored or if many of them are off task doing something else, such as playing with objects in their desks, writing notes to their friends, or talking to each other. When the instructional pace is too fast, students have difficulty keeping up. They may not be able to answer questions when you pose questions to the group or they may make many errors if they are trying to work problems with you. Pay attention to body language. If your students look confused (blank stares) or frustrated, your pace may be too fast.

Turn Desks Around to Prevent Students from Playing with Items in Their Desks. Desks that have openings facing the students are often distracting to them. By turning their desks around, students will need to walk to the front of their desk or reach over their desk to have access to the items in their desks, resulting in fewer distractions.

Teach Students to Self-Monitor Their On-Task Behavior.   Self-monitoring can improve students' ability to stay on-task while engaging in academic tasks (Harris, Friedlander, Saddler, Frizzelle, & Graham, 2005). When teaching students how to self-monitor on-task behavior, use the following instructional sequence.

- Write an observable and measurable definition of on-task behavior.
- Model examples and nonexamples of on-task behavior.
- Provide opportunity for the student to practice the behavior. Provide feedback and correction.
- After the student demonstrates on-task behavior, teach the student how to monitor and record on-task behavior. Model the method for monitoring and recording the behavior (e.g., tapes with sound prompts, verbal prompts, visual prompts, or tactile prompts). An example of a tactile prompt is having the student wear a buzzer that is set to go off at random times so he or she can monitor whether he or she is on task at those times.
- Allow the student to practice monitoring and recording on-task behavior. Provide feedback and correction.
- Initiate the self-monitoring program when the student demonstrates understanding of the process.

A lesson plan for teaching students how to record on-task behavior is included in Appendix A. Figure 1.10 provides an example of a self-monitoring data collection sheet.

Minimize Distractions with Appropriate Seating.   Identify environmental distractions and seat students with disabilities away from windows, air conditioning units, doors, and other things or people that could divert their attention away from learning activities.

Name: _____   Date _____

Self-Monitoring Data Collection Sheet

<u>On-task behavior:</u> *Writing when the class is writing, reading when the class is reading, responding when the class is responding.*

<u>On task also includes:</u> *Sitting with pockets on the seat, both feet on the ground, hands/feet to self.*

When the teacher asks, mark whether you are ON TASK. Mark a + if you're on task. Mark a 0 if you are off task.

Minutes	1	2	3	4	5
On/Off					
Minutes	6	7	8	9	10
On/Off					

<u>Off task is:</u> *Talking to a neighbor, calling out or talking out, playing with objects on or in the desk, doing anything other than writing, reading, or responding when the class is writing, reading, or responding.*

<u>Off task is also:</u> *Being out of your seat, touching someone else, not facing forward in your seat, or sitting with your feet up on the chair or desk.*

FIGURE 1.10   On-Task Data Collection Sheet.

Eliminate Potential Distractions in the Classroom Environment.   Classrooms can be fun, engaging environments in which to learn. However, too much noise or environmental stimulation can make it difficult for students with disabilities to focus attention. Monitor the level of noise in the classroom. If classroom noise exceeds what is reasonable for a specific activity, provide feedback and correction (OSERS, 2004). Visual distractions can be eliminated by providing study carrels or secluded study areas.

Provide Short Breaks for Physical Movement to Break Up the Amount of Time Students Must Sit Quietly.   Most students and adults have difficulty sitting for long periods of time. Build short breaks into lessons. Breaks do not have to be lengthy nor should they interrupt instructional flow. Breaks can be as simple as allowing students to get out of their seats to return books to a book shelf or to put completed assignments in a basket on the teacher's desk.

Provide Positive Reinforcement for Staying on Task.   Sometimes it is easier to notice when students are off task than to notice when they are on task. When students are on task, help them to learn that being on task is appropriate behavior by specifically praising the behavior. For example, say, "Wow, Allison, I'm so pleased to see you doing your work. You're developing good work habits." If you use a token economy system in your classroom, give students tokens for staying on task and for completing assignments.

Use Small-Group Instruction.   When students with attention deficits are instructed in small groups, it is easier for them to focus their attention because there are fewer distractions. Incorporate small-group instruction in instructional plans. To optimize opportunities for learning, develop small-group lesson plans that elicit high rates of student response and promote engaged learning.

Suggestions for Culturally or Linguistically Diverse Students

Culturally and linguistically diverse students may have very different backgrounds in terms of previous school experience. Some students may have attended school regularly, and others may have had little opportunity for formal schooling. In addition, perceptions of school and learning may differ. For example, in some parts of Argentina, students in grades K–12 attend school for four hours a day. It is not uncommon for students and teachers to miss school without experiencing negative consequences. Consequently, some immigrants from Argentina may have different perspectives about attendance and attending to instruction than students from other cultures.

Learning a new language creates challenges for students from diverse cultures. It takes time and effort to learn a new language. Even when students have a functional understanding of English, processing academic language can be difficult. When students have to process more language than they can easily understand, they may tune out or mentally disengage.

To address the instructional needs of students who are culturally or linguistically diverse, teachers should create learning environments that promote active, engaged learning and that are at the same time culturally responsive. Students are more likely to focus attention when teachers require participation in learning activities and when activities validate students' existing knowledge and experience. Additionally, teachers should adapt how they use language to accommodate the needs of ELLs.

Provide Culturally Responsive Instruction.   Culturally responsive instruction incorporates the everyday concerns of students into the classroom curriculum. When students' everyday lives do not parallel school experiences, culturally responsive lessons make new subject matter irrelevant and insignificant. Lessons that are relevant to students' experience are more likely to capture student interest and attention (Padron et al., 2002). For example, some ELLs enrolled in school are the only members of their families who speak English. A lesson that includes literature about interacting in two different cultures could capture students' attention and interest if the material is relevant to their lives.

Teach Vocabulary Associated with Attention Using Role-Play Situations.   ELLs may appear to not attend or pay attention merely because they do not understand the rules or demands being asked of them. This may necessitate teaching the meaning of "pay attention," "watch me," "stay in your seat," or any request the teacher may make. Role play examples and nonexamples of these phrases so students can better grasp their meaning.

Monitor and Adapt Speech for ELLs.   Not only may students not attend because they don't understand teacher requests, they generally will not have acquired the academic language necessary to understand the content being taught. Evaluate how you use language and adapt your language to meet the needs of ELLs.

- Break complex sentences into short, simple sentences.
- Explain idiomatic expressions, or avoid using them when instructing. For example, students from other cultures may not understand the following expressions: *by and large, beside the point, chime in*, and *back to the drawing board*. When using idiomatic expressions, check for understanding.
- Pause often to allow students to process what they hear.
- Restate instructions at a slower rate when needed.
- Use simple, everyday language to explain key words or technical vocabulary (McLaughlin & McLeod, 1996).

SOCIAL COMPETENCE

Schools are social environments where students interact with teachers, staff, volunteers, and peers. Students must develop social competence in order to successfully function in school environments. Social competence is defined as the ability to select and carry out interpersonal goals that lead to social fulfillment (McCay & Keyes, 2002). The term implies being able to judge the quality of one's own performance (Prater, 2007). To have social competence, students must demonstrate independence, social sensitivity, friendship-building skills, assertiveness, and social problem-solving skills—all of which are important for social fulfillment at school (McCay & Keyes, 2002).

To function successfully in school, children need to learn how to interact appropriately with those in authority, such as their teachers, paraeducators, and other school personnel. When they engage in meaningful learning activities, complete their work independently, and manage their behavior, they enhance these relationships.

Students must also interact appropriately with peers to function successfully in school. Because a significant amount of classroom learning involves interacting with peers, students need to be socially sensitive, understand the feelings of others, and respond to social cues in order to form satisfying social relationships. As students develop friendships with peers, assertiveness is necessary for communicating social needs and for protecting oneself from social harm. Most students will encounter some social problems at school. An inevitable part of growing up is learning how to cope with social challenges. Social problem solving is necessary for resolving conflict, making responsible choices, handling harassment, and for successfully collaborating with others.

To become socially competent, students must acquire and use specific social skills. Social skills are measurable, interpersonal behaviors that enable students to competently perform social tasks (Prater, 2007). Table 1.10 presents social skills associated with each area of social competence.

TABLE 1.10   Social Skills

SOCIAL COMPETENCE	SPECIFIC SOCIAL SKILLS
Independence	■ Following directions ■ Completing assignments ■ Setting goals
Social Sensitivity	■ Sharing ■ Recognizing the feelings of others ■ Expressing feelings
Friendship Building	■ Smiling and laughing with peers ■ Inviting others to play ■ Apologizing
Assertiveness	■ Standing up for oneself ■ Resisting peer pressure ■ Asking for help
Problem Solving	■ Avoiding trouble ■ Making a decision ■ Responding to teasing ■ Negotiating

Source: McCay & Keyes, 2002; McGinnis & Goldstein, 1997.

Possible Difficulties with Social Competence

Most "typical" children acquire skills needed to develop social competence. Students with disabilities, however, often manifest deficits in social functioning (McCay & Keyes, 2002). This could be due to a number of different factors. Individuals with cognitive or perceptual deficits may have difficulty processing social information. When students have language or communication impairments, they may not send or receive accurate social messages (Prater, 2007). For example, if a student with a language impairment is asked if he or she is cold, the student might misinterpret the question and answer, "No, I don't have a cold."

In addition, students with disabilities may not interact with nondisabled peers frequently enough to enable them to learn how to behave appropriately. Because students with disabilities lack skills to know how to interact competently with peers, they often withdraw from social interactions and isolate themselves. The student who does not know how to play with peers at recess may sit alone on the playground. Any time a student with disabilities isolates himself or herself, the student has fewer opportunities to learn how to appropriately interact with peers.

When students with mild to moderate disabilities are included in general education classes, teachers will most likely observe some inappropriate behaviors. Students with attention and emotional disorders are often impulsive. They may blurt out answers, interrupt conversations, cut in line, or abruptly leave in the middle of an activity (Prater,

2007). Their peers may perceive them as impulsive and inattentive. "Perseveration" can be a problem for students with lower cognitive ability and students with autistic spectrum disorders because they can get stuck and persist in an activity or conversation when it is no longer appropriate to continue the activity or conversation. Transitioning from one activity to another can be problematic for some students, as is being flexible in responding to the needs or concerns of peers.

Accommodations and Adaptations that Address Social Competence Difficulties

Teachers can provide classroom support for students who demonstrate social deficits. A supportive classroom environment and explicit social skills instruction can help students with disabilities learn and understand social boundaries.

Explicitly Teach Classroom and School Rules.   Children need to understand that there are boundaries for behavior. These are reflected in both school and classroom rules. The following is a list of guidelines for establishing classroom rules (Prater, 2007).

- **Develop rules at the beginning of the school year.** Establish classroom rules during the first few weeks of the new school year and refer to the rules throughout the school year.
- **Allow students to help establish classroom rules.** Students assume more ownership of rules when they have helped to create them. Provide opportunity for students to help develop classroom rules.
- **Behaviors described in rules should be observable and measurable.** If the rules are observable and measurable, then it is easier for students to understand the desired behavior. The rule "be nice" is ambiguous. Instead, define appropriate behavior by stating, "Hands and feet to self."
- **Rules should be stated in positive terms.** By stating rules in positive terms, teachers teach appropriate behavior rather than emphasizing inappropriate behavior. "Don't get out of your seat" should be written as "Ask for permission to leave your seat."
- **Rules should be posted.** Post rules so that students can remember them and teachers can refer to them during the school day.
- **Establish and teach consequences for keeping and breaking rules.** Teach consequences as you teach the rules. When consequences are known and understood by teachers and students, teachers can consistently deliver specific consequences. In addition, when positive and negative consequences are posted with the rules, the teacher and students can expect greater consistency with their previously determined consequences.
- **Periodically review rules and revise if necessary.** As you implement rules and consequences, it may be necessary to revise rules to make them clearer or to change rules that are difficult to enforce. Solicit student input when revising rules.

Clearly Explain Behavior Expectations for New Situations.   Because students with disabilities may not accurately perceive social cues, it is important to explain behavior expectations for new situations. At school, students learn that they have to stay with their class and their teacher as they walk through the hall. At the zoo, however, a curious child may forget the rule and may wander off to explore something of interest. Always state rules and behavior expectations for new activities and situations.

Review Class Rules or Behavior Expectations Prior to Engaging in Transitional Activities.   Sometimes it is difficult for students to shift attention from one activity to another. At the end of one activity, and prior to engaging in a new activity, clearly explain behavior expectations so that it is easier for students to make transitions. This is particularly important when students are engaged in a preferred activity and they have to transition to a less preferred activity, such as coming in from recess or physical education (PE) to start math. Before leaving the PE field, review expectations for entering the classroom and for starting math work. Make explanations clear and direct such as, "Class, when you walk in the classroom, sit down quietly at your desks until I give you instructions for math."

Establish Predictable Routines.   Students with mild to moderate disabilities may behave inappropriately when they have unanticipated changes in their environments. Establish predictable routines (e.g., turning in homework, coming in from recess, transitioning from one subject to the next) so that students can anticipate what is expected of them throughout the school day.

Post and Follow a Predictable Daily Schedule.   A posted schedule helps students anticipate activities and can help them behave appropriately during transitions (see Figure 1.11). Referring to the schedule and checking off completed activities helps students reduce their anxiety and social misbehavior because they are more able to anticipate upcoming tasks and expectations.

Conduct Role Plays to Ensure that all Students Understand Rules.   It is often easier for students with disabilities to understand behavior expectations when appropriate behavior is demonstrated rather than explained. Demonstrate or role play examples and nonexamples of appropriate behavior so that students can compare and contrast appropriate and inappropriate behavior.

Class Schedule—8th Grade English	
■ 8:30–8:45	**Literacy Journal**
■ 8:45–9:30	**Reading Selection**
■ 9:30–9:45	**Response Groups**
■ 9:45–9:50	**Assignments**
■ 9:50	**Bell**

FIGURE 1.11   Class Schedule.

Provide Many Opportunities for Students to Practice Appropriate Behavior.   After teaching new rules it is important to provide opportunities for students to practice appropriate behavior and to receive feedback and correction if necessary. One way of doing this is to assure that the student knows the expectations for various environments. For example, teach the student the explicit and implicit rules for different subjects such as math, reading, science, and socials studies and in different locations such as on the PE field, in the lunchroom, and in the computer lab.

Reinforce Desired Social Behavior by Praising Students and by Providing Tangible Reinforcement for Appropriate Behavior.   When you praise specific behaviors, students learn what you expect of them. Say, "I like how you shared the crayons with your partner," to communicate the expectation that students share in the classroom and to reinforce appropriate behavior. If a token economy system is used in the classroom, post the reinforcement schedule for specific behaviors. A token economy is a behavior management technique that involves determining appropriate classroom behaviors, teaching students expected behaviors, and giving students tokens when they demonstrate desired behaviors. For example, if you teach students to bring their materials to class, give them tokens each time they bring their materials. The tokens students earn can be exchanged for various reinforcers such as computer time, a piece of candy, or even a homework pass. Figure 1.12 is an example of a reinforcement schedule for appropriate social behaviors.

Teach Students How to Self-Monitor Their Social Behavior.   Students can be taught to self-manage social behavior. If a student forgets to ask permission to borrow items from a peer, teach the student how to ask for permission before taking another person's property. Also, teach the student to track how often he or she asks before taking something (see Figure 1.13). Then, provide reinforcement for the appropriate behavior and for self-monitoring behavior.

Provide Corrective Feedback for Social Behavior.   When students behave inappropriately, correct the inappropriate behavior by teaching appropriate behavior rather than criticizing the child. For example, if a student does not comply with instructions, state the inappropriate behavior (e.g., "You did not follow instructions") and re-teach

REINFORCEMENT FOR APPROPRIATE BEHAVIOR	
Bring materials to class	2 tokens
Follow directions the first time asked	2 tokens
Stay in seat when working	1 token
Ask for help when needed	1 token

FIGURE 1.12   Reinforcement Schedule.

How to Ask for Something

Look at the person.
Say, "May I borrow_____?"
Wait for the person's answer.
If yes, take the item and say thank you.
If no, say, "Maybe I can borrow it some other time?"

Self-Monitoring:

□ I followed the steps to ask for something.
□ I didn't follow the steps to ask for something.

FIGURE 1.13   Self-Monitoring Example.

appropriate behavior. "When I give instructions, look at me, and then do what I ask quickly." After re-teaching the appropriate behavior, provide several opportunities for the student to practice the behavior. Reinforce when the student demonstrates the appropriate behavior.

Suggestions for Culturally or Linguistically Diverse Students

Students from other cultures may have different views of what it means to be a student or to participate in the learning community. Some students may feel uncomfortable asking questions or participating in classroom discussions if asking questions is considered disrespectful in their culture. The nature of classroom discussions can differ for various cultures. In Hawaii, Hawaiians often use *talk story*, which is talking to one another about whatever is on one's mind. It is not rude to overlap speech in a way that others would consider impolite.

Nonverbal communication styles can also vary across cultures. Southeast Asian students may smile when they are happy, sad, being reprimanded, or not understanding (Sileo & Prater, 1998). Teachers who are unaware of this cultural difference may view the smile as a challenge or as disrespectful behavior. It is important to be sensitive to cultural differences and to explicitly teach expected behaviors. Teachers should work with family members and others to identify differences in your social/behavior expectations and the students' cultures.

In addition, for immigrant children it is especially important to teach students expected classroom and societal behaviors. At the same time, teachers need to show sensitivity by protecting the new student from any potentially unkind behavior from other students and by highlighting the new student's culture. Teachers should express positive values in whatever appears "foreign" to the other students. "Present the newcomer's music, food, dress, and other surface values that can be seen, while learning to appreciate the deep cultural values that can present potential conflicts" (Ariza, 2006, p. 15). The following accommodations can help students from diverse cultures understand social and behavior expectations.

```
Classroom Rules

English
Turn in completed assignments.
Follow the teacher's directions.
Work when you are supposed to work.
Keep hands and feet to self.
Bring materials to class.

Spanish
Entrega tus tareas completadas.
Sigue las direcciones del maestro.
Trabaja cuando debe estar trabajando.
Mantiene tus manos y pies.
Trae las materials a la clase.

Chinese

繳交完成的作業
聽老師的話
該做功課時,做功課
不要動手動腳
記得帶上課要用的東西
```

FIGURE 1.14   Examples of Rules in English, Spanish, and Chinese.

Post Classroom Rules and the Daily Schedule in the Language of the Students.   When rules are posted in students' native language they do not have to mentally translate the rules when they need to read them (see Figure 1.14).

Use Pictures Next to Classroom Rules.   Pictures help students remember the classroom rules without having to process language. Post pictures next to classroom rules.

Remember that What Is Reinforcing May Be Different for Students from Different Cultures.   Do not assume you know what reinforces students, particularly those from diverse cultures. Consult with the parents or others of similar cultures regarding reinforcement. What is considered reinforcement in his or her culture is only effective when the person receiving the reinforcement perceives it as something positive. For example, public praise may be perceived as reinforcing by some students but be considered embarrassing by others. Native American cultures teach modesty about their achievements and may not feel comfortable with praise or with being singled out for recognition. Reinforcement surveys are valuable for all students. These could be given to ELLs in their native language.

Use Body Language to Augment Speech.   Students will rely on nonverbal cues and gestures while learning the new language. When transitioning from one activity to another, point and make gestures to show students where they need to go. Holding up a book or demonstrating how to fold a paper helps students follow directions as you provide verbal instructions.

MOTIVATION AND ATTRIBUTION

Motivation plays an important role in academic achievement. When students are motivated to learn, they generally listen to instruction, keep attention focused on academic activities, participate in classroom discussions and activities, complete assignments, and expend effort to meet and exceed teacher expectations (Okolo, Bahr, & Gardner, 1995). Some students demonstrate these behaviors because they are intrinsically motivated, meaning their motivation comes from within. Intrinsically motivated students tend to be curious; they want to learn, have a desire to succeed, and engage in academic activities to achieve personal goals (Prater, 2007). Other students may be extrinsically oriented. They work to achieve external rewards that are meaningful to them such as grades, privileges, and status. Factors that influence motivation include (a) students' ability to perform tasks, (b) whether students perceive learning activities as relevant and interesting, and (c) students' beliefs about their ability to learn (Okolo et al., 1995).

Closely related to motivation is attribution style. Attribution style is defined by how individuals attribute success or failure to factors within and beyond their control. If students attribute or explain their success in terms of their effort and ability, they focus on their internal qualities. They believe that success is directly related to what they do, and they expect that their effort will enable them to achieve success in the future. In contrast, when students attribute success only to external factors, they may believe that their success occurred because of luck or chance. For them, success is perceived as unpredictable, random, and unexpected.

Possible Difficulties with Motivation and Attribution

Students with mild to moderate disabilities often lack motivation for learning and attribute academic performance to factors outside themselves. As stated above, motivation is impacted by students' ability to perform tasks. If students lack skills necessary for completing academic work, it is easy to understand why they would not want to engage in some activities. For example, a student who comfortably reads material written at a third-grade level would struggle significantly if asked to read material written on a sixth-grade level. Over time, if the student's skills do not improve as academic demands increase, such difficulties can adversely affect motivation.

Students' interest in academic activities can also influence motivation. Students with disabilities are like other students; they have their own interests and are often motivated to participate in activities that align with their interests. A student who loves animals might be eager to contribute to discussions about mammals or a student who is fascinated by cars might independently learn about cars. Although students with mild to moderate disabilities have interests that motivate them to learn, their range of interests may be narrower than other students and they may not perceive some learning experiences as relevant to their lives. The student who loves to build may spend hours working on a science project that involves construction but may completely lack motivation for writing an essay or composing a poem. Academic achievement can suffer when students do not have enough interest in assignments to sustain them through completion.

Attribution style is another factor that impacts motivation to engage in academic activities. When students experience failure often enough, they may attribute failure to "the stupid class," "the unfair teacher," or even to their disability. And they may quit trying because they believe that their effort does not matter. On the surface it may seem as though these students are lazy and just need to try harder. The reality is, however, frequently failing decreases motivation to engage in challenging tasks and distorts students' perceptions of their ability to learn. They don't expend effort because they believe it will not make a difference.

Accommodations and Adaptations that Address Motivation and Attribution

Being positive and encouraging with students who have experienced failure helps them develop confidence to engage in academic activities. Accommodations that address motivation and attribution involve teaching students how to learn and how to manage their learning behavior.

Create a Classroom Environment that Is Positive and Supportive—Catch the Students Being Good.   Throughout the school day, provide praise and reinforcement for all attempts at improving. Give lots of verbal and nonverbal reinforcement. Verbal praise can be general, such as "good job," "well done," and nice work"; or praise can be specific, such as "These are well-written paragraphs" and "Great job reading the entire page." Specific praise is more likely to result in reoccurrence of the particular behavior you are hoping to see increase.

Establish and Communicate High Expectations for all Students.   Having high expectations means holding students accountable for learning while providing the support students need to succeed at academic tasks (Stipek, 2006). To communicate high expectations, pay attention to students' work and provide constructive feedback; do not accept halfhearted effort; provide assistance when students need help; and refuse to give up on students. When holding students accountable for their academic and social behavior, it is important to provide necessary support and encouragement. Without appropriate support, students may become discouraged or feel alienated rather than being motivated to learn and succeed (Stipek, 2006).

Merely having high expectations for student performance is not sufficient, however. Teachers must communicate their expectations for student performance. Students with disabilities may not understand expectations that are implicit or not directly stated. Clearly explain expectations for academic work and for social behavior. For

TABLE 1.11   Essay Guidelines

ESSAY GUIDELINES	EXPLANATION
Length	■ Two to three double-spaced pages. ■ Twelve-point font.
Organization	■ Use headings for each section: Introduction, Discussion, and Conclusion. ■ Introduction: One paragraph. Introduce the topic and explain your position. ■ Discussion: Include three to five paragraphs. In each paragraph write an introductory statement for the paragraph and provide examples that illustrate your main points. ■ Conclusion: One paragraph. Summarize what you have written and state your conclusions.
Writing Mechanics	■ Center the title. ■ Center the headings. ■ Indent each paragraph. ■ Follow rules for capitalization and punctuation. ■ Proofread your work or have someone else proofread your work for you.

example, if you ask your students to write an essay about technological advances of the past decade, provide guidelines that clearly communicate your expectations for the assignment (see Table 1.11). Explicitly teach expectations for classroom behavior. Table 1.12 provides examples of social behaviors.

Provide Rewards or Incentives for Completing Necessary Tasks when Students Appear Unmotivated.   If you observe that a student lacks interest for completing certain

TABLE 1.12   Classroom Behavior Expectations

SOCIAL BEHAVIOR	WHAT TO TEACH
Classroom Routines	■ Procedures for entering and leaving the class (e.g., whether to leave when the bell rings or wait for the teacher to excuse students). ■ Procedures for submitting homework.
Personal Belongings	■ Rules for possessing and using electronic devices. ■ Where to put personal items such as backpacks and coats.
Obtaining Assistance in Class	■ Guidelines for getting help from the teacher, such as raising hand or walking up to the teacher's desk. ■ How to ask peers for help.

assignments, provide incentives that motivate the student to complete the work. In selecting rewards or reinforcers, use the least-powerful reinforcer that accomplishes the desired effect (Okolo et al., 1995). For example, if a student will write ten spelling words to earn a smiley-face sticker, do not offer the student ten minutes of free time for writing all the words.

Scale back on the reinforcement or increase performance demands as soon as possible. Instead of giving the child a sticker every time he or she writes ten words, give the child a sticker every other time he or she completes the assignment. Or, have the student write fifteen words to receive the same reinforcer.

Older students will also respond to age-appropriate reinforcement. Junior high and high school students might work to earn bonus points, assignment passes, or classroom privileges such as computer time and free time. The principles discussed above apply to older students: use the least-powerful reinforcer possible and scale back when students improve performance.

Use Choice to Promote Self-Regulated Learning.   Allowing choices has been shown to increase on-task behavior and productivity and has been associated with generalization of learning. During study and work completion time, allow students to choose what work to do and when to do it. Choice cards are one way to promote choice (Mithaug, 2002) (see Figure 1.15). When using choice cards, students are asked to plan what they will do during a study session. Before making choices about completing work, students use their work folders to review their worksheets and assignments. They decide how they will spend their time, mark their decisions on their choice card, and begin working for a specified period of time. At the conclusion of the work session, students mark whether they met their goal, which helps them learn that they are capable of setting and achieving short-term goals.

| Name: _____ | | | |
| Date: _____ | | | |
Set Goal	Assign Work	Complete Work	Meet Goal
Science	What I will do_____	What I did_____	Yes/No
Reading	What I will do_____	What I did_____	Yes/No
Math	What I will do_____	What I did_____	Yes/No
Social Studies	What I will do_____	What I did_____	Yes/No
Writing	What I will do_____	What I did_____	Yes/No

Number of "Yes" response circles? _____
Points Earned?   _____

FIGURE 1.15   Choice Cards.

Source: From "'Yes' Means Success: Teaching Children with Multiple Disabilities to Self-regulate During Independent Work" by D.K. Mithaug, *TEACHING Exceptional Children, 35* (1), 2002, 22–27. Copyright 2002 by the Council for Exceptional Children. Reprinted with permission.

Teach Students that Their Effort, Knowledge, and/or Skills Impact How Well they Do.   Plan instruction that helps students make the connection between effort, application of skills and strategies, and performance (Prater, 2007). If students lack skills for completing specific academic assignments it will be difficult for them to make this connection. Assignments should be at students' instructional levels and homework should be at students' independent levels. A student's instructional level is the level at which he or she has the prerequisite skills necessary for learning new information. An independent level of learning is the level at which the student no longer requires instruction and can complete assignments independently.

Encourage Students to Set Effort and Performance Goals.   Help students learn how to set reasonable short-term goals for completing classroom work and assignments. For example, ask students to set goals for how many problems they will finish within a specified period of time. Or, have them plan how much time they will spend working on an assignment (Fulk & Montgomery-Grymes, 1994). This is particularly important for secondary students who often have large projects to complete. If students are encouraged to plan how much time they will spend working on their projects each day, it is easier for them to make progress and complete assignments (see Table 1.13).

Provide–Performance Related Feedback.   Appropriate feedback can enhance performance. Feedback should be frequent, clear, constructive, and encouraging (Fulk & Montgomery-Grymes, 1994). Because students with disabilities may not attribute their performance to their effort, feedback should be provided that encourages effective learning. Telling students to try harder is not helpful. Instead, encourage students to follow steps or to use specific strategies when solving problems. For example, a teacher could say, "Follow the steps on the prompt sheet for solving addition and subtraction word problems." If students make errors, teachers should correct the errors as soon as possible so that the students do not practice making mistakes. (For example, "It looks like you're skipping the second step, let's go back and try that again without skipping the second step. Great job reworking the problem!")

Encourage Students to Track and Monitor Their Progress.   Seeing progress can help motivate students. Create progress-monitoring sheets that enable students to quickly

TABLE 1.13   Assignment Planning

ASSIGNMENT: HORIZONS PROJECT	TARGETED COMPLETION DATE AND NUMBER OF DAYS TO COMPLETE
Article Review	April 10th: two days (one article/day)
Interview	April 14th: one day
Current Issues	April 19th: two days
Research Note Cards	April 20th: four days (five note cards/day)
Research Report	April 28th: five days (one page/day)

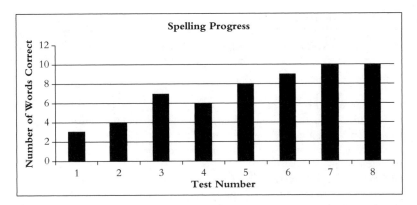

FIGURE 1.16 Example of Progress-Monitoring Sheet: Spelling Graph.

and easily see how their performance is improving (see Figure 1.16). When charting students' performance, remember to respect students' right to privacy concerning grades. Develop systems that allow individuals (not their peers) to track classroom performance.

Provide Prompts to Reduce Student Errors.   When students are taught concepts and skills and then taught how to apply their knowledge, they are less likely to make errors. Reducing errors and failure can increase motivation. When teaching new skills, provide prompts that guide students through problems and procedures (see Figure 1.17).

Promote Self-Determination so that Students Become Responsible for Their Own Learning and Behavior.   Instruction that promotes self-determination should begin early for students with disabilities. They need to be taught how to set goals, solve problems, and evaluate their performance if they are to become motivated learners (Palmer &

ADDING THREE-DIGIT NUMBERS WITHOUT RENAMING

1. Read the problem out loud and circle the sign.
2. Start with the ones column.
   a. Say the top number
   b. Say plus
   c. Say the bottom number
   d. Write the answer under the ones column.
3. Add the tens column. Repeat a–d for the tens column.
4. Add the hundreds column. Repeat a–d for the hundreds column.

FIGURE 1.17 Math Prompt.

TABLE 1.14   Self-Determined Model of Instruction

THE SELF-DETERMINED LEARNING MODEL OF INSTRUCTION

Phase 1—Setting a Goal
Questions
1. What do I want to learn?
    Student identifies instructional needs, communicates preferences, and prioritizes needs.
2. What do I know about it now?
    Student identifies current status and gathers information about opportunities and barriers to learning.
3. What must change for me to learn what I don't know?
    Student decides how to direct action: toward capacity building, modifying the environment, or both.
4. What can I do to make this happen?
    Student states a goal and identifies the criteria for achieving the goal.

Phase 2—Taking Action
Questions
5. What can I do to learn what I don't know?
    Student evaluates current status.
6. What could keep me from taking action?
    Student determines a plan of action to bridge the gap between self-evaluated status and goals.
7. What can I do to remove these barriers?
    Teach student-learning strategies necessary for achieving learning goal.
8. When will I take action?
    Assist the student in scheduling and implementing action.

Phase 3—Adjusting the Goal or Plan
Questions
9. What actions have I taken?
    Help student self-evaluate progress toward goals.
10. What barriers have been removed?
    Collaborate with the student to evaluate progress.
11. What has changed about what I don't know?
    Help student revise plans if necessary.
12. Do I know what I want to know?
    Have student evaluate outcomes.

Source: From "Promoting Self-determination in Early Elementary School: Teaching Self-regulated Problem-solving and Goal-setting Skills" by S. B. Palmer and M. L. Wehmeyer, *Remedial and Special Education, 24* (2), 2003, 115–126. Copyright 2003 by PRO-ED, Inc. Reprinted with permission.

Wehmeyer, 2003). *The Self-Determined Learning Model of Instruction* (see Table 1.14) can be used to teach students self-determination skills (Palmer & Wehmeyer, 2003). The model is implemented in three phases: setting goals, taking action, and adjusting goals or plans. In each phase, students ask themselves questions that guide them through goal-setting and problem-solving processes.

Use Instructional Methods that Prevent Students from Making Errors While Learning. Anticipate errors students will make and design instruction that prevents students from making errors. Incorporating cognitive strategies in instruction is one way to reduce student errors. Cognitive strategies are a series of steps students follow to solve problems (Stein, Kinder, Silbert, & Carnine, 2006). They should apply to a reasonably broad range of problems, and using the strategy should enable students to complete work without making errors. For example, when learning about fractions, students often experience difficulty in understanding improper fractions. Initially, they tend to think that fractions represent numbers less than one. To prevent errors and misconceptions, teach students that the denominator is the number of parts in each group, and the numerator is the number of parts that are shaded. As students learn the concepts, they are given proper and improper fractions to work with to prevent them from forming misconceptions (Stein et al., 2006).

Lower the Affective Filter so that Students Will Be Willing to Take Risks. An "affective filter" is a guard to protect oneself from any kind of harm, including emotional harm such as embarrassment or failure. Trying new things can be intimidating for students who have experienced school failure. Anxious students may need encouragement to take risks and to try new activities (Okolo et al., 1995). If students make mistakes as they learn new skills, help them to understand that making mistakes is part of the learning process.

Teach Students How to Handle Failure. We all make mistakes when we are learning new information or acquiring new skills. Use failure as an opportunity to teach students about resiliency. Although effective teachers provide errorless learning opportunities, some students will still occasionally experience failure because teachers do not control everything that occurs in students' lives. Students may fail at hitting the softball with a bat, spelling all words correctly on a spelling test, or initiating a conversation with a peer. When students experience failure, teach them to focus on improving their performance in the future. Help students identify the reasons they may have failed and to generate ideas for improving performance. Then, teach them how to select a course of action to improve performance (McGinnis & Goldstein, 1997).

Create Interest in Learning New Material by Explaining the Relevance or Rationale. Students can quickly perceive whether teachers are interested in the material they are teaching. Student motivation can be heightened by teachers' interest and excitement. When teaching new skills or information, explicitly explain the rationale. Help students understand how academic learning is used in daily living. For example, writing skills are necessary for completing job applications, and basic math skills are important when figuring discounts for items on sale in a store.

Suggestions for Culturally or Linguistically Diverse Students

As discussed previously, motivation for learning is influenced by students' ability to perform tasks, their personal interests, and their beliefs about their ability to learn.

If students do not have skills necessary for learning, their skill deficits create significant learning barriers. This is particularly true for students of lower economic status, who often lack the skills necessary for learning. According to Payne (2003) "the true discrimination that comes out of poverty is the lack of cognitive strategies. . . . The supports these students need are cognitive strategies, appropriate relationships, coping strategies, goal-setting opportunities, and appropriate instruction both in content and discipline" (p. 139).

The same is true for culturally and linguistically diverse students. They face challenges other students do not face (i.e., learning academic material in a new language and understanding a new culture), and they may doubt their ability to acquire academic skills. Teachers need to provide accommodations that support learning and help students calibrate self-efficacy with their ability to learn.

Incorporate Cooperative Learning Activities in Classroom Instruction.   For culturally diverse students, cooperative learning activities allow them to communicate with peers and to develop social, academic, and communication skills as they learn new content. These skills are important because as students improve their ability to contribute to the classroom-learning climate, self-confidence and self-esteem are enhanced. When students feel safe participating in classroom activities, motivation for learning can increase (Padron et al., 2002).

Enrich Instruction with Assistive Technology.   Providing assistive technology can be particularly helpful for students who are learning English. For example, if students struggle to process academic language in written texts, they may avoid reading. Providing access to digitized books or text-to-speech software are two ways to provide support students may need to experience success in reading books in English. With digitized books, students can request pronunciations for unknown words and translations of sections. They can even ask questions about what they are reading. When learning is supported, students are more likely to be motivated to learn (Padron et al., 2002).

Incorporate Cognitive Strategy Instruction in Lessons.   If students lack strategies for learning new information, they may experience failure, which can negatively impact motivation for learning. Teachers can incorporate cognitive strategies in lessons. Cognitive strategies are strategies learners use to learn or process new information. Teaching students how to identify the main idea of a reading selection is a comprehension strategy that can be incorporated in science, social studies, health, and reading lessons.

PART II

ACCESSING GENERAL EDUCATION CURRICULUM

Before Marcus entered school, his parents were concerned about his ability to learn. They noticed that things other children could do, such as focus attention during preschool lessons, carry on conversations with others, and remember information, were difficult for Marcus. Because of their concern, Marcus's parents had him evaluated for a LD. The test results indicated that Marcus did have a LD.

As difficult as it was for Marcus's parents to accept the diagnosis that their child had a LD, they did all that they could do to ensure that his educational needs were met at school. They wanted Marcus to be taught grade-level curriculum and to have opportunities to interact with his peers. Throughout his years in the public school system, Marcus's parents worked with teachers to plan and implement supports that would enable him to make progress learning grade-level curriculum. The support he received in general education classes helped him make academic progress. When he was eighteen, Marcus graduated with his peers and received a standard diploma.

When the Education for All Handicapped Children Act (EAHCA) was passed in 1975, the intent of the law was to provide students with disabilities with the same opportunities for public education that their nondisabled peers were afforded. Before the law was enacted, many students with disabilities were excluded from public education or were not receiving appropriate public education; the law was passed to remedy discriminatory practices (Rothstein, 2000). The guiding principles of the EAHCA (later renamed the Individuals with Disabilities Education Improvement Act [IDEA, 2004]) are (a) students with disabilities cannot be excluded or rejected from public education, (b) evaluation procedures should be nondiscriminatory, (c) education programs are individualized to meet students' needs, (d) students with disabilities should be educated with their nondisabled peers to the maximum extent appropriate, (e) due process procedures protect students' rights, and (f) parents and students participate in making educational decisions.

According to IDEA (2004), students with disabilities are entitled to a free and appropriate public education. Case law has defined appropriate education as specialized instruction designed to provide educational benefit to students with disabilities. When students with disabilities are included in general education classes, their individualized education programs (IEPs) should be reasonably calculated to enable the students to achieve passing marks and to advance from grade to grade (Rothstein, 2000). In order for this to occur, however, support must be provided to allow the students to access and learn the general education curriculum. Without appropriate support, students with disabilities may not benefit from being included in general education classes.

In this section, we discuss instructional accommodations and adaptations that can help students with disabilities access general education curriculum. Specifically, we address accommodations and adaptations that help students access instruction and printed information, learn new material, remember what they've learned, complete assignments, and work with others.

ACCESSING CURRICULUM AND INSTRUCTION

Curriculum and content standards originate from two sources. First, professional organizations such as the National Council of Teachers of Mathematics generate content standards for content area subjects. Second, state and local school boards make curriculum decisions that impact what teachers teach in classrooms. Although these decisions are made outside teachers' classrooms, teachers determine what they will teach each day. In deciding what to teach, the question of "depth or breadth" is important to consider. Professional organizations compile extensive lists of standards that often include more topics than teachers can reasonably cover during one school year. Yet, students develop a greater understanding when teachers thoroughly examine subject matter rather than providing a superficial treatment of a broad range of topics. In fact, current research indicates that focusing on fewer topics is more likely to improve student achievement (McTighe, Seif, & Wiggins, 2004). The challenge for teachers then, becomes one of identifying and teaching critical content, and teaching it in enough depth to facilitate learning and understanding.

Not all students demonstrate the same levels of academic achievement. Thus, assessing students' instructional needs is a critical aspect of planning instruction. Assessment information should be used to establish goals and objectives that align with students' instructional needs. For example, if students are expected to master basic math facts but do not know how to count objects, counting skills need to be taught first. Similarly, if the students in the class have already mastered basic facts, then they are ready to learn new skills.

Teachers' methods of instruction impact whether students meet specific learning objectives. There are many methods for delivering instruction (e.g., lecture, demonstration, explicit instruction, inquiry learning, and problem-based learning), all of which elicit varying degrees of student engagement and interaction. Researchers have reported that student engagement is one of the most important variables in terms of learning outcomes. For students to be actively engaged in learning, (a) the learning activities must directly relate to the material being taught, (b) tasks should be at an appropriate level for the students' stage and level of learning, and (c) the task or activity should be structured so that students experience a high degree of success (Prater, 2007). Teaching methods that promote engaged learning involve asking students questions, teaching strategies for completing work and solving problems, providing opportunities for peer interaction, and teaching critical thinking skills, among others.

Possible Difficulties with Accessing Curriculum and Instruction

When classroom instruction moves at a fast pace and a large number of topics are covered during the school year, students are often expected to be independent, self-sufficient learners. Students with mild to moderate disabilities may experience difficulty managing their own learning if they lack the skills and strategies needed to keep pace with instruction. Consequently, they may not acquire the content or meet standards (Lenz, Ehren, & Deshler, 2005).

If students with disabilities have not acquired grade-level academic skills, there may be a mismatch between the students' instructional needs and the levels at which instruction is provided in inclusive classrooms. A sixth-grade student who reads at a fourth-grade level needs to be taught fourth-grade reading skills. Instruction at sixth-grade levels would create frustration for the student. When instruction is not presented at levels at which students can experience success, students with disabilities can lose motivation to engage in learning activities, and they may develop inappropriate behaviors. To avoid reading assignments that are too difficult, a student may talk with peers, put his or her head down, or refuse to read.

Sometimes, students with disabilities withdraw and do not participate in class. Traditional practices, such as requiring students to raise their hands to speak and calling on students to read in round-robin fashion often engage only a few learners at any given time (Feldman & Denti, 2004). In many cases, students with disabilities are among the students who do not participate when teachers call on individuals rather than asking for responses from all learners (Feldman & Denti, 2004). This may be because the students lack confidence to contribute to class discussions, or they might be distracted by other things going on in the classroom environment when they are not actively participating in learning activities. Teachers may notice that some students appear to be off task or not attending to instruction. They may talk with peers, play with things in their desk, or get out of their seats when they are not actively engaged in learning. When students with disabilities do not actively participate in learning activities, it is less likely that they will learn the content being taught.

Accommodations and Adaptations that Address Problems Accessing Curriculum and Instruction

To help students with mild to moderate disabilities access instruction, adapt the classroom curriculum and adapt how instruction is delivered. Design curriculum to promote learning for all students, embed learning strategies in instruction, and use teaching methods that promote active, engaged learning.

Design Curriculum Around Instructional Priorities and "Big Ideas" that Help Students Acquire New Knowledge.   Instructional priorities are skills or concepts that are critical for academic learning. For example, by the end of first grade, beginning readers should be able to read words with three to four sounds, read three-to-four-letter words fluently, answer literal comprehension questions, and retell simple stories. First-grade curriculum should be structured to address these instructional priorities (Kame'enui & Simmons, 1999). Curriculum for all grades and content areas should be designed to cover instructional priorities. For students with disabilities, it is especially important that they acquire basic skills. By structuring curriculum to focus on critical concepts and skills, students are more likely to acquire academic skills necessary for progressing in school.

Even when critical content is taught, students with disabilities may experience difficulty in constructing knowledge. Designing instruction to include "big ideas" helps students make sense of what they are learning. "Big ideas" are overarching themes or principles. They capture relationships among concepts, form the basis for generalization, and involve ideas and principles central to higher-order learning. As an example, in social studies, *securing liberty* is an idea that can span an entire course of study. When studying the history of the United States from early settlements through the Civil War, historical events such as establishing colonies, the Revolutionary War, and the Civil War can be discussed in terms of how individuals sought liberty. When students examine how the circumstances surrounding one event (e.g., colonizing America to establish religious freedom) relate to conditions that precipitate other events (e.g., the Revolutionary War fought to secure political freedom) they can better make the connections necessary for synthesizing learning.

Provide Instructional Support or Scaffolding to Enable Students to Experience Success in Meeting Learning Objectives.   Instructional scaffolding is intended to eliminate problems students might have in understanding new information or acquiring new skills by providing support at the students' current level of understanding. As students master new skills and acquire independence, support can then be removed. There are many ways to provide scaffolding or instructional support, such as (a) sequencing skills from less complex to more complex, (b) teaching material such as the letters "p" and "d" that could be easily confused on separate occasions, (c) providing illustrative examples, and (d) providing process prompts (Kame'enui & Simmons, 1999) (see Table 2.1 and Figure 2.1).

Explicitly Teach Students Steps for Accomplishing a Goal or Task.   Students with disabilities may lack skills for breaking tasks or goals into manageable steps. Provide step-by-step instruction for meeting goals or completing tasks (Kame'enui & Simmons, 1999). Figure 2.2 is an example of step-by-step instructions for writing a research report.

Teach Students How to Relate What They're Learning to Previously Learned Information.   Students learn new information easier and more quickly when new information is connected to prior knowledge. When introducing new material,

TABLE 2.1 Examples of Instructional Scaffolding

ACADEMIC SKILLS OR TASKS	LEVEL OF UNDERSTANDING	SCAFFOLDING
Reading consonant sounds	Students cannot read consonant sounds.	Use pictures that depict how the sound is produced as it is read.
Writing the letters *b* and *d*	Students can write the letters *a* and *s*. Students have difficulty discriminating direction (right or left).	These letters can be easily confused; introduce them during different lessons.
Write the letter *a*	Students can draw straight and curved lines but have difficulty forming letters correctly.	Use a prompt sheet. Start with tracing the letter *a* and then move to independently writing *a*.
Reading from left to right	Students can read vowel and consonant sounds. They have difficulty starting at the beginning sounds of a word and reading all sounds from left to right in order to read the word.	Draw an arrow pointing to the right under words the students are decoding.
Subtracting fractions with different denominators	Students can subtract fractions with like denominators.	Provide numerous examples that illustrate the process.
Dividing fractions	Students can multiply fractions and can write the reciprocal of fractions. Students become confused when they have to sequence through a number of steps to solve a problem.	Highlight the fractions that need to be changed to the reciprocal. Explicitly teach the steps for dividing fractions.
Writing a sentence with a compound subject	Students can write sentences with simple subjects.	Teach students how to write a sentence with a simple subject before teaching students to write sentences with compound subjects.

help students make connections by explicitly explaining relationships among concepts or by prompting students to make connections. For example, if students are learning about good health practices and have studied the benefits of exercise to promote health, help them connect healthy eating as another way of practicing good health. Concept maps are helpful for visually representing relationships (see Figure 2.3).

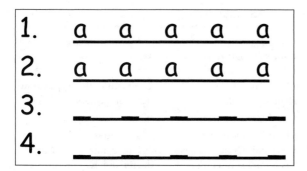

FIGURE 2.1   Prompt Sheet for Writing the Letter *a*.

Writing a Research Report

1. Research the topic on the Internet. Find two to three articles.
2. Print the articles and read each article.
3. Write four to five main ideas from each article on 3 × 5 index cards. Write the citation for the article on the back of each note card.
4. Organize and group the note cards by themes or topics.
5. Take each group of cards and write one to two paragraphs that summarize the information on the cards.
6. Write an introduction for the paper.
7. Put the paragraphs in logical order and write transition sentences to connect paragraphs.
8. Write a conclusion.
9. Proofread the paper. Make necessary corrections.
10. Submit the draft for feedback.

FIGURE 2.2   Writing a Research Report.

Incorporate Review and Recall Activities in Lessons.   As discussed in Part I, students with mild to moderate disabilities may have memory deficits. Review is particularly important to help students solidify learning. When planning units and lessons, structure instruction to always include some amount of review.

Teach Prerequisite Skills and Information.   Most of what we learn builds on previous knowledge or skills. Students learn how to hold pencils before they can write their names, they learn how to write sentences before they can write paragraphs, and they learn how to multiply before they divide. Assess students' skills and teach prerequisite

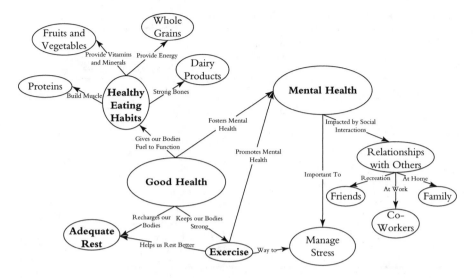

FIGURE 2.3   Good Health Habits Concept Map.

skills necessary for learning critical content. Table 2.2 illustrates prerequisite skills necessary for writing a research report, and Table 2.3 illustrates skills necessary for writing letters of the alphabet.

Provide Instruction at Students' Instructional Level.   Assess your students' skills to determine instructional needs, and then provide instruction at students' instructional levels. A first-grade student who has difficulty holding a pencil and forming written

TABLE 2.2   Prerequisite Skills

WRITING A RESEARCH REPORT	
SKILL	**SOME PREREQUISITE SKILLS**
Locating articles on the Internet	Conducting an Internet search. Discriminating whether information is from a good source.
Writing the main idea on a 3 × 5 index card	Comprehending and summarizing a passage. Writing the main idea in a complete sentence.
Writing a paragraph about a subtopic	Writing complete sentences. Organizing and writing a paragraph.
Writing a three-page essay	Ordering and organizing paragraphs in a logical manner. Writing introductory and concluding paragraphs.

TABLE 2.3   Prerequisite Skills for Writing Letters

PENMANSHIP	
SKILL	SOME PREREQUISITE SKILLS
Write letters *a, c, d, g, o, q,* and *s*	Hold a pencil. Write on paper. Draw a straight line. Write on a line. Draw a curved line. Draw a circle.
Write letters *l, t, v, w, x, y,* and *z*	Hold a pencil. Write on paper. Draw a straight line. Write on a line. Draw a diagonal line.

letters is probably not ready for instruction on how to write a three-word sentence. Instruction for the student should focus on pencil grip and letter formation.

Develop Supplementary and Simplified Curriculum Goals for Students with Mild to Moderate Disabilities.   Supplementary goals can focus on remediating basic academic skill deficits such as those in reading, writing, or arithmetic. Or, goals can address self-management and social skill issues. For example, a student with a reading disability might have a supplementary curriculum goal to improve basic decoding skills. A self-management goal might be to improve the student's ability to stay on task when given classroom assignments.

Develop Simplified or Alternative Lesson Objectives.   Students' IEP goals should align with the general curriculum, and in a classroom lesson, all students' learning objectives can stem from a common learning standard. From the common standard, adaptations can be made for students with mild to moderate disabilities. Simplified lesson objectives should match a student's instructional level and focus on either lower grade-level skills or on basic concepts and useful skills. Table 2.4 illustrates how lesson objectives can be simplified or adapted for students with disabilities.

Use Choral or Group Responding to Involve all Students.   Choral and group response provides a safe environment for practicing new skills and helps all learners to keep attention focused on instruction. When asking for a group response, allow students time to think, and then provide a cue for the response. The cue can be a verbal cue, such as "Ready, recite." Or, the cue can be nonverbal, such as pointing at a word or problem when you want students to respond. To illustrate, if you are teaching students how to read new sight words, show your students the word "which" and then prompt

TABLE 2.4 Alternative Lesson Objectives

LESSON OBJECTIVES	EXAMPLES
A science lesson objective	When asked to illustrate the nitrogen cycle, students will draw a representation of the nitrogen cycle and will use scientific terms to describe each part of the cycle.
A lesson accommodation	Given a word bank of words that describe the nitrogen cycle, students will put the words in order to reflect the cycle.
A simplified lesson objective	Given a word bank of words that describe the nitrogen cycle and given a graphic organizer that outlines the cycle, students will arrange the words in order on the graphic organizer.
An adapted lesson objective	Given a word bank of words that describe the nitrogen cycle and given a graphic organizer that depicts the cycle, students will match words with pictures that illustrate the cycle.

Source: Janney and Snell, 2006.

them to look at the word and to think about how to read it. After providing think time, give the students a cue (such as pointing to the word on the overhead projector) when you want them to read the word together. If all the students read the word correctly, move on to the next word. If students read the word incorrectly, re-teach the word and provide more practice before moving on with the lesson (Feldman & Denti, 2004).

Use the Thumbs Up Strategy to Encourage all Students to Formulate Answers to Questions. After asking a question, tell your students to put their thumbs up when they know the answer. Remind them not to blurt out their answer, and be sure to provide thinking time. Then, call on students randomly or cue the students to respond chorally or as a group (Feldman & Denti, 2004).

During Class Discussions, Use the Think-Pair-Share Strategy to Involve all Students. The think-pair-share strategy is a good strategy to use when asking open-ended questions that have many possible answers. Pose an open-ended question. Ask students to form pairs and to share their answers with their partners. Then, call on students to share their responses with the class.

Teach Students How to Utilize e-Resources. Information found on the Internet can be useful when teacher or peer support is not available. Teach students to use the Internet to address background knowledge gaps (Silver-Pacuilla & Fleischman, 2006). For example, Ask For Kids (http://www.askforkids.com) is a web site students can access if they have questions about academic subjects. Students type in a question or a search request and are then directed to resources that answer their questions.

Suggestions for Culturally or Linguistically Diverse Students

Students from diverse cultures may experience difficulty in responding to classroom curriculum. Much of what we learn depends on prior knowledge, and if students come from a culture other than the dominant one the curriculum may not align with the students' prior knowledge, values, or interests. In addition, students' experiences with oral language can differ according to culture. In some cultures, parents engage their children verbally to a high degree and expect their children to demonstrate comprehension using oral language skills. In other cultures, the emphasis is on doing rather than explaining (Chamberlain, 2005). Culture clash can occur when teacher expectations for student response in the classroom differ from students' cultural experiences. The following suggestions can address issues related to culture clash.

Learn About Your Students' Backgrounds. Learn about your students' lives outside school. This can help you to develop instruction that is responsive to their needs. When instruction matches students' interests, students can become more motivated to learn new information. In addition, gather information about the students' academic history. This will enable you to make appropriate decisions about classroom curriculum and instruction (Finnan, Schnepel, & Anderson, 2003).

Build Positive Student-Teacher Relationships. Close relationships with teachers can lead to higher levels of student engagement and achievement (Stipek, 2006). Make efforts to show personal interest in students. Give compliments, listen to students' concerns, be positive, greet students when they enter the classroom, and show an interest in students' lives outside school.

Select Curriculum that Is Culturally Familiar. Students who are learning English and who represent diverse cultures may experience anxiety as they encounter cultural differences at school. Reduce student anxiety by developing lessons that are relevant and culturally familiar. Students who live in inner-city neighborhoods might relate to lessons about city life; or, it might be important for immigrants to see the accomplishments of people from their country mentioned or highlighted in class. Integrate culturally significant material in the classroom curriculum.

Adopt an Integrated Approach to Instruction. An integrated approach involves contextualizing explicit-instruction lessons to make them relevant for culturally diverse students (Chamberlain, 2005). To be authentic, curriculum must be linked to the world outside the classroom and to what students already know (Finnan et al., 2003). Explicit instruction methods often involve transmitting knowledge to students—that is, the teacher explains or models new information, and students acquire knowledge as the teacher presents it. When using explicit methods, contextualize instruction in ways that make learning meaningful for students from diverse cultures. For example, as you explicitly teach basic math skills, emphasize that math skills are important for making purchases at local markets or for counting change to ride the bus. Use pictures of items sold at local markets to help students understand how school learning is part of their lives.

Students learning English as a second language may need more opportunities to discuss ideas and to explore new learning than explicit instruction methods typically provide. Integrate interactive questions and discussions in lessons. Interactive questions and discussions between students and the teacher provide opportunities for students to use academic language in an academic setting. During discussions, take time to understand and inquire about the students' cultural perspectives. Because of cultural differences, students may respond to questions in ways teachers do not expect. Different responses do not necessarily mean incorrect responses (Chamberlain, 2005). If, for example, a teacher asks students to describe an egg and a student says that an egg is something he eats on Sunday when his grandmother comes to dinner, the student's response is not incorrect given the student's cultural perspective of the topic. The student is describing the egg in functional (how eggs are used) and relational (people at his home when eggs are eaten) terms. Another student in the classroom might say the egg is white, oval, and fragile, which reflects a concrete, physical description of the egg (Chamberlain, 2005). Considering culture, one response is not more correct than the other. Both students described the eggs in ways that reflected their cultural perspective.

Encourage all Students to Contribute to Class Discussions.   Students' backgrounds can significantly influence how they respond in an academic setting. Students who live in poverty may not have the same opportunities for socialization as do other students. They may not be as confident in contributing to class discussions or in sharing their opinions, and, when asked a question, may refuse to respond or may give one- or two-word responses. English language learners (ELLs) may be reluctant to use their language skills in front of the whole class. Encourage reluctant talkers by repeating the last few words of the student's response, followed by the word "and" (Glazer, 1996). The following dialogue illustrates this technique.

> **Student:** I have a dog.
> **Teacher:** You have a dog, and ...?
> **Student:** I have a dog and he's really cute.
> **Teacher:** "He's really cute and ...?
> **Student:** He likes to lick my face.

When Reviewing Previously Learned Information, Use the Tell–Help–Check Strategy to Provide Opportunity for all Students to Check Their Knowledge.   Students who are learning English are less likely to actively participate in classroom review activities (Feldman & Denti, 2004). The tell-help-check strategy is a robust strategy for ensuring that all students review critical information. The strategy is similar to the think–pair–share strategy in that students pair up and work together. Assign students to work with a partner and designate which student is student "one" and which is student "two." Pose a close-ended question (a question that has one correct answer). Give the students think time and then have student one share what he or she knows with student two. Student two then adds additional information and elaborates, or corrects what student one shared. Finally, both students check their notes, the textbook, or the overhead to see if they correctly answered the question (Feldman & Denti, 2004).

ACCESSING PRINTED MATERIAL

A significant amount of classroom learning involves processing printed material. Teachers use books, textbooks, workbooks, overheads, and handouts to present information to students. Most students develop skills that enable them to process printed material; they can read what's printed, they understand what they read, and they learn how to construct knowledge from printed text so that reading becomes a meaningful activity for them.

Textbooks play a stronger role in students' education as they get older and progress through school. In secondary grades, in particular, textbooks are used in many core classes, and students need to know how to extract information from textbooks in order to access course curriculum. Text processing skills include reading headings and using text cues to locate important information, understanding the meaning of new vocabulary, analyzing visual material such as charts and graphs, and summarizing paragraphs and passages.

Possible Difficulties with Accessing Printed Information

Many students with mild to moderate disabilities experience difficulty in learning to read. Often, their reading achievement lags behind their peers and they do not possess the reading skills necessary to comprehend grade-level material. Reading problems generally fall into three categories: (1) word analysis deficits, (2) comprehension deficits, and (3) word analysis deficits and comprehension deficits. Students use word analysis skills to decode new words and to analyze complex words (i.e., break words into syllables). Students with word analysis deficits have difficulty decoding new words and reading multisyllable words. Comprehension is the ability to understand written text. Sometimes students can accurately read printed words but fail to understand what they are reading. Finally, some students with disabilities experience difficulty in reading and comprehending new material.

In addition to reading skill deficits, students with mild to moderate disabilities may encounter problems identifying important information from textbooks. Some textbooks are complex and provide more information than students need to learn. Students with disabilities may have difficulty filtering through information presented in a chapter and determining what is important and relevant. They may get bogged down in the details presented on the page and may fail to identify important information.

Accommodations and Adaptations that Address Problems Accessing Printed Information

To address reading problems and problems processing text information, accommodations should aim to help students access information they need to learn. Accommodations that address these issues include providing support for reading, using assistive technology, and teaching students strategies for processing text information.

Explicitly Teach Text-Structure Strategies to Show Students How to Locate Important Information and How to Find Information to Answer Questions About the Material Covered in Class. Textbooks usually have a specific organization or structure. Five commonly used expository text structures include the following: main idea structure, list structure, order structure, compare and contrast structure, and classification structure (Bakken & Whedon, 2002).

When teaching text structure strategies, first teach the students how to identify each structure. After students can discriminate among different structures, teach them how to use specific strategies for each structure. Table 2.5 illustrates strategies for the five structures. Then, provide an opportunity for students to practice taking notes that they will use for studying. For students with mild to moderate disabilities it is important to model new skills, guide their practice, and provide feedback and correction as they learn how to recognize and discriminate different structures and to take notes.

Read Aloud to the Class. In addition to helping students to access information, reading aloud aids students in building vocabulary and oral language skills. When reading aloud, make sure that students have their text in front of them, and encourage them to follow along as much as possible. Periodically ask questions to assess whether students comprehend what you are reading. Read with expression and discuss the meaning of new vocabulary (Bakken & Whedon, 2002).

Assign a Peer to Be a Reading Buddy. If a student understands the text when it is read to him or her, assigning a peer buddy to read passages is an option for text access. When you assign a peer buddy to read to a student with disabilities, be careful to assign a student who will treat the student with respect, and while the students are reading, evaluate how the student with a disability responds to the situation. If it embarrasses the student to have a peer read to him or her, consider other options, such as asking for adult volunteers to work in the class, or arranging for older students to read with him or her.

Use Text-to-Speech Technology. Students with disabilities often experience difficulty in decoding words. When they make numerous errors reading words, their ability to comprehend passages can be significantly impacted. This occurs because they are using their cognitive resources to decode words rather than for comprehending meaning (Forgrave, 2002). With text-to-speech programs, text is entered into a speech synthesis program. Students can instruct programs to read selected words, phrases, or the entire text. The use of text-to-speech programs helps reduce frustration associated with

TABLE 2.5 Strategies for Analyzing Textbooks

EXPOSITORY TEXT STRUCTURE	STRATEGIES FOR THE STRUCTURE
Main idea	1. Look for definitions, principles, and laws. 2. State the main idea in your own words and list three supporting points.
Lists	1. Look for semicolons, numbers, or letters in parentheses. 2. Restate the general topic and list four characteristics of the idea.
Order	1. Look for words that signal order such as first, second, then, and finally. 2. State the general topic and describe steps in the sequence.
Compare/Contrast	1. Identify words that indicate a comparison is being made (e.g., in contrast to, the difference between). 2. State the general topics being compared and discuss what is the same or different about them.
Classification Structure	1. Determine how the information is being classified. Phrases such as *can be classified*, *are a group*, and *these are types* indicate classification. 2. List characteristics of different classifications.

Source: From "Teaching Text Structure to Improve Reading Comprehension" by J. P. Bakken, and C. K. Whedon, *Intervention in School and Clinic*, 37 (4), 2002, 229–233. Copyright 2002 by PRO-ED, Inc. Reprinted with permission.

inaccurately decoding, and facilitates comprehension. Microsoft Word and Excel have text-to-speech features that are easy to use.

For young readers and ELLs, use digital storybooks to help students engage in reading stories. Older students can download texts as e-books that they can read with text-to-speech (Silver-Pacuilla & Fleischman, 2006).

Provide Audio Access to Text Material.   Electronic audio files, tapes, or CDs of texts can be used to help students to access written materials. You can make your own tapes or obtain audio materials from commercial companies. The Recording for the Blind and Dyslexic Organization offers a wide variety of audio texts (www.rfbd.org). When making a tape recording of a text, follow the guidelines listed below (Dyck & Pemberton, 2002).

1. Make the tape in a quiet place.
2. Mark the textbook to let the student know how to follow along in the book. For example, if material is omitted on the tape, indicate omissions in the text.

3. Provide directions such as: "Turn to page 15 and look at the chart on the top of the page."
4. Discuss illustrations, maps, charts, and graphs following the paragraphs where they are mentioned.
5. Integrate text usage and study skills in the recording. This can be done by prompting the student to preview the chapter before listening to the rest of the recording.

Reduce the Amount of Material to Read. If a student can read the text but reads at a very slow rate, it may be appropriate to reduce the amount of material the student is required to read. Mark or highlight key passages to indicate what the student should read. Realize, however, if the learning objective is to improve reading skills, reducing the amount to be read may not provide students with enough practice to improve reading ability.

Support Reading. The support reading strategy is similar to text structure strategies in that the teacher adds cues or signals that help students to learn how to find information in the textbook. Highlight titles and headings, underline important words, or put signals in the margins that indicate where important information is discussed in a passage (Dyck & Pemberton, 2002).

Provide Graphic Organizers that Illustrate the Structure of the Chapter or Section. A one-page graphic organizer is easier for students to understand than an entire chapter of print. Give students graphic organizers before they read a section or chapter. The organizer becomes a preview of the material and activates student attention on important elements of the section (Dyck & Pemberton, 2002). Figure 2.4 is an example of a hierarchical organizer that alerts students to important information.

Provide an Alternate Text, but Be Certain it Teaches the Same Concepts. When selecting an alternate text, evaluate the structure of the text by asking these questions. Is the text easy to follow? Is the structure clear? Does the text provide clear explanations of concepts? Although the reading level of some alternate textbooks may be a better match for students who struggle to read grade-level material, not all textbooks are easy to read or follow. Some textbooks contain extraneous information or visuals that detract from reading and learning the concepts presented. Select textbooks that have clear, logical organization and match the students' reading skills and knowledge.

Suggestions for Culturally or Linguistically Diverse Students

The printed word is emphasized more in Westernized cultures than it is in cultures that value oral-language traditions (Chamberlain, 2005). Coming into the classroom, students from diverse cultures and students who live in poverty may not have the same exposure to books and printed texts as other students (Hadaway et al., 2004). For them, learning from printed material may be difficult because they have not had experience in learning from texts.

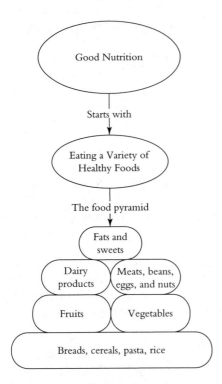

FIGURE 2.4   Chapter Organizer.

Students who are learning English may also experience difficulty reading academic material. If students are learning English, their ability to read academic language may not be at the same level as their ability to speak or understand conversational English. They may need classroom accommodations that address challenges reading classroom material.

Provide Supplemental Reading and Audiovisual Materials.   Provide access to books that cover the same content covered in class but that are written at different reading levels. To meet the needs of diverse learners, it is important to provide reading material at the students' instructional levels. If books are too easy, students do not learn anything new, if books are too hard, then accessing the information is beyond the students' grasp (Hadaway et al., 2004). Assess students' reading skills and provide access to books they can read. In addition, use DVDs/videotapes or let students use interactive CDs that cover the same material included in classroom textbooks.

Provide Opportunities for Students to Activate Prior Knowledge.   Before beginning a chapter, teach students to examine chapter headings and discuss what they know about chapter topics. Encourage students to make predications about what they will read. Predictions and prior knowledge can be discussed orally or written down (Sheppard, 2001).

Provide all Materials From Which Students are Expected to Access Information.
Students living in poverty may not have access to supplementary materials such as
magazines, dictionaries, or the Internet. Also, do not assume that students have access
to the public library. Immigrants and families who live in poverty typically do not
know about this community resource or how to access it.

LEARNING INFORMATION

When teachers' instruction is responsive to students' instructional needs and they provide materials that are accessible to students who have problems reading, opportunities
for learning are created. The next challenge is to help students learn what is being
taught. Students learn course or grade-level curriculum as they attend class and receive
instruction. Learning takes place as students engage in learning activities associated
with daily lessons. Over time, learning accumulates and students build knowledge
structures.

The process of constructing knowledge involves identifying what is important
to learn, and then using strategies to facilitate learning. Effective, efficient learners have
good attention skills, and they develop strategies for learning. Strategies are tools, plans,
or methods for accomplishing tasks (Beckman, 2002). Students who excel at learning
use a variety of strategies that enable them to learn. Table 2.6 describes five types of
learning strategies.

Possible Difficulties with Learning Information

As discussed in the concept formation section, students with mild to moderate disabilities often experience difficulty in learning new concepts. It is difficult for them to
make connections and to construct knowledge. Unlike other students who can construct the "big picture" from information presented, students with mild to moderate
disabilities have problems understanding how parts relate to the whole. They may read
a story and fail to see how a sequence of events develops a broader theme; or, when
learning addition and subtraction, they may have problems understanding that addition and subtraction are inverse operations.

Along with having difficulty in constructing knowledge, learning new information is challenging for students with disabilities because they have problems with
attention and they often lack strategies for effective learning (Prater, 2007). In order to
identify essential information to learn, students need good filtering skills. Students'
attention deficits make it difficult to identify important information from chapters or
units of instruction. They can become overwhelmed when they have to read large sections of text. Their answers to comprehension questions may reflect problems in identifying main points and critical information. For example, if asked to name the most
significant battle in the War of 1812, a student might write the name of the first battle
she finds as she looks through the chapter. It might be difficult for her to sift through
the information about the battles to determine which battle is the most significant.

TABLE 2.6 **Five Types of Learning Strategies**

STRATEGY	DESCRIPTION
Cognitive Strategies	■ Visualization: Creating mental images ■ Verbalization: Self-talk ■ Making associations: Connecting new learning with prior knowledge ■ Questioning: Asking questions to activate attention ■ Chunking: Condensing and categorizing information ■ Underlining: Identifying important information
Learning Strategies and Cues	■ Following specific steps or procedures to accomplish a task ■ Using visual or verbal prompts to recall information or to learn new information
Goal Setting and Self-Monitoring	■ Setting personal achievement goals ■ Monitoring work and behavior ■ Asking questions and clarifying
Self-regulation Strategies	■ Planning how to complete tasks and managing and Metacognitive Strategies learning behavior ■ Being aware of how one learns and using that knowledge to learn new information and skills
Task-specific Strategies	■ Mnemonic: Devices for remembering information ■ Reading: Strategies for accuracy, fluency, and comprehension ■ Writing: Strategies for planning, revising, questioning, checking, and monitoring

Source: Beckman, 2002.

Generally speaking, students with disabilities do not use effective learning strategies. Most likely, they do not engage in self-talk when solving math problems, they have difficulty in creating and articulating visual images of stories, they struggle to begin and complete assignments, and they are not cognizant of what they need to do to learn new information.

Accommodations and Adaptations that Address Problems Learning New Information

For students with disabilities it is important to design instruction that helps them to construct knowledge, identify important information, and that also teaches them how to learn. Below we discuss adaptations that support learning.

Use Unit Organizers to Give Students a Preview of What They Will Learn. When planning instructional units, identify what the students should know or understand at the conclusion of the unit, how students will demonstrate their understanding and knowledge, and what skills or enabling knowledge students need to achieve the unit objective (Prater, 2007). With that information, develop a unit organizer. Unit organizers are graphic organizers that provide a preview of what will be learned. They should describe information to be learned, activate prior learning, include main ideas and supporting ideas, illustrate how ideas and concepts are related, list unit questions, and provide the schedule for completing the unit (Boudah, Lenz, Bulgren, Schumaker, & Deshler, 2000). An example of a unit organizer is provided in Appendix B.

Provide Students with a List of Learning Objectives, New Vocabulary to Be Learned, and the Concepts and Skills to Be Learned.   By providing this information to students, it is easier for students to focus their attention on what they need to learn. Learning objectives can address material covered during a unit, during one week of instruction, or even in a single lesson. Figure 2.5 is an example of this type of instructional support.

Provide a Study Guide to Help Students Learn as they Complete Assignments.   Study guides focus students' attention on what they need to learn. Guides should align with learning objectives and should only cover information in a chapter that is important for students to learn. Providing guides help students to identify relevant information in reading material. Figure 2.6 illustrates how a study guide aligns with the learning objective in Figure 2.5.

Incorporate Learning Strategies in Instruction.   As you teach students new information, also teach them strategies for learning the information. Incorporate learning strategy instruction in your lessons. Table 2.7 provides examples of learning strategies that can be incorporated in lessons.

When teaching strategies, use the following instructional sequence.

1. Describe the strategy. Explain the rationale for using the strategy, and tell the students when and how to use the strategy.
2. Model how to use the strategy. Explain each step of the strategy.
3. Allow students to practice the strategy and to provide corrective feedback if necessary.
4. Promote self-monitoring and strategy use. If students see the benefit of the strategy, they will be more likely to use it. Encourage them to monitor their performance.
5. Prompt students to continue to use the strategy after initial instruction. Encourage generalization (Beckman, 2002).

An example of a strategy lesson plan is included in Appendix A.

If Lecturing, Give Students Guided Notes to Help them Take Notes on Class Lectures.
Guided notes are developed by the teacher prior to the lecture and reflect the structure of the lecture (Boyle, 2001). As the teacher verbally presents information, students write down information in the space provided in the notes. Guided notes are usually two to

---

RIVERS
What We Will Learn This Week

Learning Objectives

    1. Label the parts of a river.

    2. Draw an illustration of a river running its course.

    3. Describe how rivers impact surrounding geography.

New Vocabulary Words

    1. source

    2. course

    3. bank

    4. oxbow

    5. estuary

    6. mouth

    7. tributary

Concepts

Rivers are dynamic and change over time.

FIGURE 2.5   An Example of a Learning Objective Sheet.

three pages long and teachers can use overhead transparencies or PowerPoint slides that contain the main points listed in the notes. For students who have difficulty writing or taking notes, guided notes minimize writing demand. Figure 2.7 is an example of guided notes.

Teach Students How to Use Strategic Note-Taking Forms to Take Notes in Class.   Strategic note-taking forms are note-taking prompt sheets (see Figure 2.8). On these forms, students record the following information: (a) the lecture topic, (b) what they already know about the topic, (c) three to seven main points with details of the topic being discussed, (d) a description of how the ideas discussed are related, (e) new vocabulary or terms, and (f) the main points of the lecture (Boyle & Weishaar, 2001).

Study Guide: RIVERS

New Vocabulary
Define each word and write a sentence using the word.

1. source

2. course

3. oxbow

4. estuary

5. mouth

6. tributary

Illustrate Rivers
Using the example on page 215, illustrate the course of a river that begins in the mountains and ends at the ocean.

Rivers Change Geography
List and discuss 5 ways that rivers change geography.

1.

2.

3.

4.

5.

FIGURE 2.6 Study Guide that Aligns with Learning Objectives.

Suggestions for Culturally or Linguistically Diverse Students

Students who are learning a second language often exhibit problems learning the new language. They may have difficulty in comprehending or expressing their thoughts using academic language, their vocabularies may be limited, and when they speak or write they may make grammatical or syntactical errors (Sheppard, 2001). If students are not proficient in English, learning becomes challenging. Teachers need to be cognizant

TABLE 2.7   **Learning Strategies**

STRATEGIES	EXAMPLES
Productivity Strategies	■ Verbalization: Talking self through procedures and steps ■ Self-monitoring: Monitoring on-task behavior ■ Using cues: Using samples, illustrations, and prompts to complete work
Memory Strategies	■ Mnemonic devices: Keywords, acronyms, rhymes, pegwords ■ Making associations: Associating something known with the information to be learned ■ Chunking: Memorizing small chunks of information
Reading Strategies	■ Accuracy: Finger tracking, decoding strategies, contextual clues, self-questioning ■ Fluency: Re-reading, partner-reading
Writing Strategies	■ Planning: Brainstorming and planning the structure of the paper ■ Writing: Structuring sentences and paragraphs ■ Revising: Editing and making corrections ■ Proofreading: Reading to check for errors

Source: Beckman, 2002.

of the challenges ELLs face in learning academic material and must adapt instruction in ways that enable students to learn what is taught, particularly when these students have disabilities.

Even if students' primary language is English, their cultural background may clash with the teacher's approach to instruction. In fact, numerous studies indicate a strong association between low socio-economic status and low achievement (Payne, 2003). Students who live in poverty, for example, may not experience the community similarly as families with higher incomes. They may not have gone to the zoo, the local museum, or have taken vacations away from home. At the same time, they are most likely more "streetwise" than other children their same age.

Students from cultural groups that promote cooperation within groups (e.g., Native American, Latino) rather than competition (e.g., European, Asian) are often at a disadvantage given the competitive nature of U.S. schools. Teachers should be cognizant of the cultural backgrounds of their students and use instructional styles to match these cultural differences.

Develop Listener-Friendly Lectures.   Listener-friendly lectures are lectures that incorporate simplified language, repetition, demonstrations, and/or modeling. They are easy

Geography-guided Notes
Weather Fronts

A. Weather and climate
   a. Weather is _____.
   b. Climate is _____.

B. Heat
   a. Most of the heat on Earth comes from _____.
   b. The warming of the earth's atmosphere near the surface helps create
      _____ and patterns of _____.
   c. _____ also contributes to weather patterns.

C. Air pressure
   a. The _____ of the atmosphere pressing down on earth is called
      _____.
   b. High pressure usually means _____.
   c. Low pressure usually means _____.

D. Weather fronts
   a. Cold fronts—cold air moves in an area of _____ air. Heavier cold air
      _____ the lighter warm air. _____ and _____ form when this
      happens.
   b. Warm fronts—_____ moves in an area of _____ air. The lighter warm air
      slides over the _____. _____ form and _____
      occurs.
   c. Stationary fronts—_____ and _____ meet but do not _____.
   d. Occluded fronts—_____ air is trapped between _____ and _____ air and
      is forced upward. _____ and _____ usually result.

FIGURE 2.7   Example of Geography-Guided Notes.

to follow and help the listener experience the content. During listener-friendly lectures, teachers use manipulatives and visual aids to help students understand by providing nonverbal clues (Sheppard, 2001). Also, teachers use scaffolding to build on students' prior knowledge (see Table 2.8).

Provide Students with Teacher-Prepared Notes.   Providing students with notes that you have created can be helpful in two ways. First, it models good note taking. Second, it gives students a clearer understanding of what you think is important. Depending on the skill level of the students, you may provide only pictorial representations, a combination of words and pictures, or words only. If necessary, use simplified vocabulary (Hill & Flynn, 2006).

Strategic Note–taking Form

Fill in this portion **BEFORE** the lecture begins.
What is today's topic?

Describe what you know about the topic.

AS the instructor lectures, use these pages to take notes of the lecture.
Topic:
Write 3 to 7 main points with details of today's topic.
    1.
    2.
    3.
    4.
    5.
    6.
    7.

Summary: Describe how the ideas are related.

New vocabulary or terms:

At the **END** of the lecture:
Write five main points of the lecture and describe each point.
    1.
    2.
    3.
    4.
    5.

FIGURE 2.8   Strategic Note-Taking Form.

Source: From "Enhancing the Note-taking Skills of Students with Mild Disabilities" by J. R. Boyle, *Intervention in School and Clinic, 36,* 2001, 221–224. Copyright 2001 by PRO-ED, Inc. Reprinted with permission.

REMEMBERING INFORMATION

As discussed in the memory section of Part I, much of school learning involves remembering—remembering facts, remembering assignments, remembering social rules, and remembering steps and procedures for solving problems. Effective learners develop and use strategies that help them to remember information. Commonly used strategies include making associations, chunking information, writing information

TABLE 2.8 Listener-Friendly Lectures

ELEMENTS OF THE LECTURE	EXAMPLES OF HOW TO MAKE THE LECTURES LISTENER-FRIENDLY
Health Class: Curriculum and units	■ Organize curriculum into thematic units. ■ Give students a chart with topics arranged in the order in which they will be covered. Each time a topic is introduced, reference the chart.
Preview: Vocabulary	■ Before beginning a lecture, have students work independently or with a partner to look up new vocabulary words. Give students a worksheet with the vocabulary words. ■ Model how to decode and read each word. Have the students repeat correct pronunciation.
Lecture Structure: Objective and questions	■ On the board, write the lesson objective and list five questions that will be answered during the lecture. ■ Instruct students to listen for key vocabulary words and point out when each question is answered.
During the lecture	■ Give students red and green circles to put on their desks. ■ If students do not understand something, they put the red circle at the top of their desk. Green indicates they understand. ■ Allow students to quietly ask a peer or paraprofessional for a translation if they do not understand. ■ Use visual aids and prompts to demonstrate lecture content. ■ Before moving from one key point to another, stop and ask questions to assess understanding. ■ Tell students what to write in their notebooks.

down, visualizing, verbalizing, and using mnemonic devices. All these strategies enhance memory and make remembering information easier.

Possible Difficulties for Remembering Information

Remembering information is often a challenge for students with disabilities. Typically, students with disabilities do not develop strategies that help them to remember information. They may forget to write things down, experience difficulty in chunking information or making associations, and they may not know how to visualize and verbalize or use mnemonic devices to remember information.

Problems with memory are particularly evident when students with disabilities take classroom tests. As students progress in school, teachers give tests to assess student achievement, and classroom tests often measure students' abilities to recall specific facts. Students with disabilities have consistently shown that they have difficulty in remembering academic content (Mastropieri & Scruggs, 1998), and poor test performance often reflects such difficulties.

Accommodations and Adaptations that Address Memory Problems

Teaching students with disabilities strategies that enhance memory is particularly important to help them remember academic content and to help them experience success when test performance significantly impacts grades. Such adaptations can be incorporated in the classroom curriculum.

Use Pictures and Encourage Visualization.   Pictures can facilitate memory (Mastropieri & Scruggs, 1998). Hang pictures on the chalkboard or use an overhead projector to project photographs or illustrations. If pictures are not available, teach students how to create their own visual image. Prompt students to add details to their visual images (Mastropieri & Scruggs, 1998). For example, if students are learning about boats, provide key words to help them construct their mental image. Tell them to think about the color of the boat, its location, size, shape, and whether it's moving.

Encourage Students to Verbalize, or to Talk About What They Are Learning.   Provide opportunities in class for students to discuss or talk about what they are learning, preferably with a partner or in small groups. If discussion groups are too large, students with disabilities may not contribute to discussions. Teach students to use their own words to describe new ideas or to restate learning. If students cannot restate what they are learning in their own words, then they do not understand and it is very unlikely that they will remember new learning.

Teach Students to Use a Strategic Note-Taking Form to Study for Tests.   The strategic note-taking form discussed in the learning information section (see page 110) can be used as a study guide (Boyle & Weishaar, 2001). After students have been taught to use the form, check their notes to ensure that they are using the form correctly. If students have accurately recorded information, teach them how to use their notes to study for tests. Teach them to cover up information to test themselves, or to use a blank form to see if they can fill in lecture information from memory.

Incorporate Concrete Learning Experiences in Instruction.   It is easier to remember facts, concepts, and vocabulary when we can relate them to concrete learning experiences. Concrete learning experiences make learning meaningful for students and provide opportunities for the content to become part of students' lives (Mastropieri & Scruggs, 1998). For example, in one sixth-grade class, a teacher brought a Skinner box to the classroom to teach students about operant conditioning. Operant conditioning is primarily concerned with the consequences of behavior and establishing relationships between behavior and consequences. The Skinner box is an experimental box for mice used to study how mouse behavior is influenced by consequences. In the box, a mouse can touch a bar (its behavior) to receive food (the consequence associated with the behavior). The students in the class, who took care of the mouse, had direct experience with the concept, and could easily remember what operant conditioning meant.

Teach Students How to Use Mnemonic Devices to Remember Information.   Mnemonic devices are systematic procedures for enhancing memory. An important aspect of learning and remembering new information is the encoding process, which is taking in information and making sense of it (Mastropieri & Scruggs, 1998). Mnemonic devices help students make sense of new information by relating what they are learning to prior knowledge (Bainbridge & Lasley, 2002). When firm connections are made, memory can last a long time (Terrill, Scruggs, & Mastropieri, 2004). The following mnemonic devices can be used to enhance memory.

- **Keywords.** Keywords involve two parts: (a) identifying an acoustically similar keyword for an unfamiliar word to be learned, and (b) using the keyword to illustrate the definition of the new word. For example, to learn the meaning of *jettison*, the key word *jet* can be used because jet sounds like the first part of jettison (Uberti, Scruggs, & Mastropieri, 2003). To remember the meaning, a picture of a jet is created with items being thrown overboard.
- **Acronyms.** Acronyms are created by taking the first letter of words to remember and forming a word such as HOMES to remember the names of the Great Lakes or FACE to remember the notes in the treble clef.
- **Acrostics.** The first letters of words of a sentence are used to remember information or procedures. The acrostic—Ninja Turtles Counting Pizza Toppings— reminds students to check their work for name, title, capitalization, punctuation, and transition words (Buchan, Fish, & Prater, 1996). Please Excuse My Dear Aunt Sally helps students remember the order of operations in math (parenthesis, exponents, multiplication, and/or division, addition and/or subtraction).
- **Rhymes.** A rhyme is a short phrase or poem used to remember information. "Thirty days hath September, April, June, and November, all the rest 31 doth rate except for February, which hath 28, and in a leap year is 29."
- **Pegwords.** Pegwords are used when numbered or ordered information needs to be remembered. Pegwords are objects that are easy to visualize and rhyme with the numbers one to ten.

"One is bun, two is shoe, three is tree, four is door, five is hive, six is sticks, seven is heaven, eight is gate, nine is vine, and ten is hen." Pegwords are used like keywords in that the pegword (e.g., one = bun) is visually associated with a keyword. As an example, if students needed to know that the first President of the United States was Washington, they would be taught the pegword for one (bun) and a keyword for Washington (washing machine). Then they would be shown a picture of buns being tossed into a washing machine to be washed. They would be asked to remember the picture and the association between one (bun) and Washington (washing machine).

Incorporate Recall Enhancement Routines in Lessons.   Recall enhancement routines are instructional routines that incorporate mnemonic strategy use in instruction. When preparing lessons, identify information that is important for students to master. Then, select a mnemonic device that is appropriate for the information to be learned and create the mnemonic. During instruction, explain what will be mastered and write the item on the chalkboard. Then, describe the mnemonic device that will be used to remember the information (e.g., keyword, rhyme, acronym) and prompt the students to write the information to be learned and the name of the mnemonic device in their notes. Next, present the mnemonic device. In subsequent lessons, review the information and the mnemonic device (Bulgren, Deshler, & Schumaker, 1997).

Promote the Use of External Memory.   External memory is using technology or other devices such as paper and pencils to record things to be remembered. As discussed in the previous section, structure classes to include time for students to write down things they need to remember such as assignments, due dates, and important content information.

Suggestions for Culturally or Linguistically Diverse Students

Culturally or linguistically diverse students can be overwhelmed with learning so much information, including a new language, content information, and a school culture, that is different from their home culture. It's not surprising that they find it difficult to remember everything. Students from culturally or linguistically diverse backgrounds especially need accommodations that help them retain what they are learning.

When Using Keywords, Select Familiar Words from the Students' First Language as the Key Word.   For example, the English word *ocean* in Chinese is *hai* which sounds similar to the English word *hi*. The meaning of hi can be illustrated by picturing a child waving hi while standing in the ocean.

Use Systematic Review to Help Students Remember Information and New Vocabulary.   Effective teachers spend five to seven minutes per lesson reviewing previously learned information (Sheppard, 2001). It is especially important to incorporate review when students are learning a new language. ELLs need to review concepts and vocabulary numerous times to retain learning.

COMPLETING ASSIGNMENTS

Learning takes effort, and part of school learning involves completing assignments during class and at home. At school, teachers provide instruction and give students assignments so that they can practice new skills or apply their learning. Teachers may prefer for students to complete assignments as groups or individually. Such assignments include papers, projects, and worksheets, as well as problem-based or inquiry learning activities.

Students may need to take work home they did not complete in class on top of assignments given specifically as homework. Homework assignments usually align with what is taught in class and provide opportunities for students to practice skills learned in class, demonstrate their understanding of content instruction, and expand on their learning (Hughes, Ruhl, Schumaker, & Deshler, 2002). Completing homework assignments is an important facet of learning and should not be used to introduce new concepts but to provide independent practice of skills already learned.

Possible Difficulties with Completing Assignments

Students with mild to moderate disabilities may encounter problems completing class work and homework assignments. Levels of academic achievement, motivation, organizational skills, memory, and attention all impact work completion. Typically, students with disabilities lag behind their peers in academic achievement, which means they may not have skills needed to complete grade-level work. For example, if students are asked to independently read a page from a social studies textbook and write a summary of the main points discussed, students would need to read the grade-level text, comprehend the passage, determine the main points, and then write complete sentences that expressed the main points covered. Students with disabilities may not have the reading and writing skills required for the assignment. In addition, students would need access to paper, pencils, word processors, and printers to complete the assignment.

When students with disabilities lack skills for completing work, they may lose motivation to work. As discussed in Part I, skills influence motivation. Becoming motivated to work is hard when you lack skills necessary for completing assignments. Attention and memory problems also significantly impact students' work habits.

Most students with disabilities will have problems with attention. Attention deficits are evident when students need to focus their attention on assignments they consider boring or uninteresting, when they have to use organizational skills to manage work completion, and when they have to attend to details associated with completing assignments. Teachers may notice that students with disabilities are frequently off task when they should be independently working. They may lose papers and assignments because of poor organization skills, or they may turn in work that is messy and incomplete because they did not pay attention to the details.

Memory deficits become a problem when students are given assignments to complete. Students with mild to moderate disabilities may not remember the instructions after they've been given if they have short-term memory deficits. They may forget to write down assignments and may also forget how to do them. Students with disabilities need repetition and practice to remember algorithms and other sequenced procedures. If they do not practice enough to learn procedures, students with disabilities may not remember how to finish or complete assignments, especially if there is a significant lapse of time between when they are taught how to do something and when they are expected to complete independent work.

The factors mentioned above not only impact whether students with mild to moderate disabilities complete in-class assignments, they also impact homework completion. Research indicates that students with disabilities may not perceive homework as being important or interesting; they may forget about assignments, quickly lose interest in homework after they start, and may need help completing homework, which may or may not be available (Bryan & Burstein, 2004; Prater, 2007).

Accommodations and Adaptations that Address Problems Completing Assignments

Students with mild to moderate disabilities need accommodations and adaptations that help them complete class work and homework. Accommodations that address skill deficits and attention, memory, and motivation problems can provide students with disabilities the support they need.

Assure that Students Have Learned the Requisite Skills for Completing Assignments on Their Own.   If students do not have the requisite skills for completing assignments, provide simplified or alternate assignments. Simplified assignments can be assignments that cover the same concepts but are not at the same level as other classroom or homework assignments (Janney & Snell, 2006). For example, if the homework assignment is twenty problems, adding and subtracting fractions with unlike denominators, a simplified assignment could be adding and subtracting fractions with like denominators.

Alternate assignments can be given if students lack skills for completing specific assignments. Students with good communication skills who have writing difficulties can be given oral rather than written assignments. Instead of assigning a student to write a five-page research paper, allow the student to present a five-minute research report.

Provide Clear and Explicit Instruction for Assignments.   Rubrics and written directions are a good way to provide clear instructions for assignments. When developing a rubric for an assignment, list all elements required and provide a description of each element (see Figure 2.9). Written directions are helpful because students can take them home and refer back to them if they forget what they need to do.

Check for Understanding by Asking Students to Repeat Directions.   If you do not check for understanding, it is easy to assume that all students know how to complete assignments. Such an assumption may not be accurate. After giving directions for class work and homework, ask students to repeat the directions together as a class or to pair up and explain the directions to a peer. If students cannot explain how to complete the assignment, re-teach the directions.

Teach Students Routines for Writing Down Assignments.   Assignment planners can be valuable tools for students. Students will, however, need to be taught how to use

---

Book Summary Rubric

In your summary, include the following elements. Each element is worth 5 points.

1. *Introduction—5 points*
   In the introductory paragraph, explain why you selected the book you read and discuss your opinion of the book.
2. *Title of the Book—5 points*
   The title should be stated in the introductory paragraph.
3. *Summary of the Plot—5 points*
   In the second paragraph, summarize the plot.
4. *Main characters—5 points*
   In the third paragraph, describe the main characters. Briefly discuss each character's personality and why each character is important in the book.
5. *Themes—5 points*
   In the fourth paragraph, discuss one theme that is developed throughout the book. Provide examples of how the theme is developed.
6. *Closing—5 points*
   In the last paragraph, provide your recommendations for other readers. Do you recommend the book? If so, discuss why. If you would not recommend the book to other readers, discuss why not.

All book reviews should be typed and proofread for errors.

FIGURE 2.9   Assignment Rubric.

planners. Specifically, teach your students how to accurately record assignments and provide time in class for students to record assignments (Bryan & Burstein, 2004; Bryan & Sullivan-Burstein, 1998).

Provide Reinforcements for Completing Homework.   Reinforce homework completion by providing students with reinforcers when they complete homework assignments (Bryan & Sullivan-Burstein, 1998). Determine the rate at which students are rewarded for completing assignments. Initially, students who struggle completing and returning assignments may need more frequent reinforcement to establish desired behavior. For an entire class, weekly rewards may be more appropriate. Once a week provide a reinforcer to all students who completed homework assignments for the week. Reinforcers can be tangibles such as snacks and items from a classroom treasure box, or they can be as simple as giving students an additional ten-minute recess on Fridays.

Give Real-Life Assignments as Homework.   Real-life assignments are assignments intended to help students to link school learning with life outside school. Assign students real-life homework to make learning meaningful, and to help motivate students to learn classroom curriculum (Bryan & Sullivan-Burstein, 1998). Real-life assignments should relate to units studied in the classroom. For example, primary students who are learning to tell time can be given an assignment to look at an analog clock and write down the time they complete specific activities such as brushing teeth, getting in bed, or eating dinner. Older students can measure their bedrooms and estimate the amount of paint needed to cover their walls.

Use Internet Programs to Post Grades for Assignments Submitted.   Many schools provide access to PowerSchool (www.powerschool.com) and other Internet sites that allow students to check their grades and their attendance records. Teach students routines for checking their progress online. Keep your record up to date so that students can track their performance.

Create Homework Graphs that Allow Students to Track Homework Completion.   A graph is a good way to help students assess and track their homework completion behavior (Bryan & Burnstein, 2004). Homework graphs can be fairly simple (see Figure 2.10). List homework assignments in each box. Instruct students to color their boxes green or another color when homework is turned in on time, yellow if an assignment is turned in a day late, and red if the assignment was not turned in. The graph not only helps students to track their performance, parents easily determine how their child is doing completing homework. With the graph, parents can quickly see if their child is completing homework, and they have specific information about which assignments have or have not been completed. They can then intervene if there are problems.

Homework Completion Graph Week of May 3–May 7				
Reading	30 Minutes of reading	30 Minutes of reading	30 Minutes of reading	30 Minutes of reading
Spelling	Copy spelling words from the book	Write words 3 times each	Write words in sentences	Write missed words 3 times each
Math	Page 13 Problems 1–15	Page 14 Problems 2–20	Page 16 Problems 1–10	Page 20 Problems 1–20
	Monday	**Tuesday**	**Wednesday**	**Thursday**

Legend
Black: On time
Grey: One day late
White: Did not turn in

FIGURE 2.10   Homework Completion Graph.

Shorten Assignments, but Provide Enough Practice Problems for Mastering New Skills.   Some students with mild to moderate disabilities may process information slowly, which means it takes them longer to complete work than other students. Teach students to record how long it takes them to complete homework assignments to gauge if the amount of homework being assigned is appropriate (Bryan & Burstein, 2004). It may be necessary to shorten some assignments for students with disabilities if they spend excessive amounts of time completing them. However, when shortening assignments, be certain to assess whether a student is getting enough practice to master skills.

Break Large Projects into Smaller, Manageable Assignments.   Some students may become overwhelmed if an assignment seems too large, particularly if they have problems with self-regulation. Self-regulation involves planning, organizing, managing time, and assembling resources necessary for completing work. To complete large assignments, teach students to (a) create a plan for completing all aspects of the project, (b) allocate time to complete each part, (c) determine what resources are needed to complete the project, and (d) assemble and use information gathered. Many students with disabilities have poor self-regulation skills and need help in planning and organizing projects. Break large projects into smaller, manageable assignments. Set due dates for parts or sections of large projects (see Table 2.9).

TABLE 2.9   Project Due Dates

STATE REPORTS	
ASSIGNMENT	**DATE DUE**
State Select the state for your report	March 4
Reference list Turn in your list of five references	March 10
Note cards Turn in twenty note cards	March 23
Rough draft Turn in three to five typed pages	March 30
Pictures and illustrations Turn in at least two pictures and/or illustrations	April 3
Final draft Turn in three to five typed pages	April 7
Report in a binder or folder Submit the completed report and include a title page, table of contents, and bibliography	April 14

Teach Students Strategies for Completing Homework.   Completing homework is more than just sitting down and doing a worksheet. Completing homework involves planning, following through, and sometimes, seeking help. Teach students how to do the following: (a) listen for and correctly record assignments; (b) plan how much time to schedule to complete assignments; (c) identify materials needed for completing homework; (d) recruit help from friends, parents, siblings, and others; (e) monitor progress; and (f) self-reward when homework is complete (Hughes et al., 2002). Some students complete the homework process but fail to turn it in to the proper location or person. Be sure to emphasize the necessity of following correct submission procedures.

Post a Visual Schedule of Due Dates in the Classroom.   In the classroom, post a schedule of due dates. Devote a spot on the blackboard to posting assignments due the next class period or the next day. In another location, post assignments that are due during the next week or month—whichever time frame is most appropriate for the age group you are teaching (see Figure 2.11).

Provide Prompt Sheets for Guides for Completing Work.   By the time students get home, they may have forgotten how to work problems or how to do their assigned homework. Prompt sheets are great tools for helping students (see Figure 2.12).

Provide an Extra Set of Books for the Student to Use at Home.   When students have organizational and memory problems, it may be difficult for them to plan which books they need to take home, organize their materials to take home the books they need for

---

Due tomorrow:

Tuesday–Spelling words written in sentences.
        Math, page 14, problems 1–20

Project due in two weeks:
Ecosystem diorama

FIGURE 2.11   Assignments Due.

Prompt Sheet for Excel 2007 Graphs

    1. Open Excel.
    2. Click on *New Sheet*.
    3. Enter classroom data.
    4. Click on *Insert*.
    5. Select the line graph.

FIGURE 2.12   A Prompt Sheet for Creating a Graph Using Excel 2007.

Name: *Steven*

From: *October 3* to *October 14*

Steven will finish math homework assignments. Completed homework assignments will be returned to school each day and will be put in the homework basket by the teacher's desk.

For turning in 9 out of 10 assignments, Steven will receive one of the following:

Five minutes of computer time   A treat out of the goodie bag   Feed the fish for 5 days

Mark the days assignments were turned in:

Monday_____ Tuesday_____ Wednesday_____ Thursday_____ Friday_____
Monday_____ Tuesday_____ Wednesday_____ Thursday_____ Friday_____

Teacher's signature _____

Student's signature _____

FIGURE 2.13   Example of a Homework Contract.

the evening, and then remember to bring the books back to school. If extra books are available in the classroom, allow students to take them home.

Create Homework Contracts.   Homework contracts with built-in rewards or reinforcers can help improve homework completion performance (Bryan & Burstein, 2004). A homework contract specifies what the student is expected to do and what the student gets when the student does what's listed on the contract (see Figure 2.13).

Suggestions for Culturally or Linguistically Diverse Students

Students from culturally and linguistically diverse backgrounds may have different perceptions of assignments. They may or may not place the same value on completing written work as the teacher, or students may lack the resources at home necessary for completing assignments. Do not assume students have access to paper, pencils, magazines, word processors, printers, and other necessary materials at home. In addition, do not assume family members can help students, particularly if they don't speak English.

When Students are Working, Circulate to Provide Help with Assignments.   Students who come from different cultures may not feel comfortable asking for help or they may lack language skills necessary for soliciting help. Make certain to circulate among the working students to provide feedback, assistance, and suggestions (Sheppard, 2001). In addition, teach students how to ask for help if they notice they are spending too much time on a task or do not understand directions. If language skills are an issue, teach students to place a need help card on their desk when they need assistance.

Explicitly Teach Students How to Meet Deadlines. Some of your students may come from cultures or live in circumstances where time is less important. Although you establish deadlines for completing and turning in assignments, students may not perceive the importance of meeting deadlines. When giving assignments, tell the students why an assignment is important and when it is due (Sheppard, 2001). Explain what support is available for completing the task, and review the steps necessary for completing the work (Sheppard, 2001). Check students' progress to gauge if they are on track for completing assignments on time.

Have High Expectations for all Students. Teacher expectations impact student performance. Evidence suggests that in schools where teachers communicate high expectations, students achieve more (Bainbridge & Lasley, 2002). Clearly communicate performance standards and the expectation that all students will complete their assignments. Outside the school community, students may not receive support and encouragement for education. Therefore, it is especially important that at-risk students know that a teacher expects them to perform well. When surveyed about their experience in school, high school African American students reported that they worked hard because their teachers encouraged them to work hard (Stipek, 2006). Along with communicating high expectations, provide classroom support that enables students to meet stated expectations.

WORKING WITH OTHERS

Learning often involves interacting with others. Informal interactions among peers such as sharing information and asking questions occur frequently in classrooms. Teachers formalize peer interactions by implementing cooperative learning and peer-mediated structures in their classrooms.

Cooperative learning is a teaching arrangement that refers to small, heterogeneous groups of students working together to accomplish a task or to achieve a goal (Goodwin, 1999). When implemented in classrooms, cooperative learning can facilitate academic learning, promote active participation in learning, and provide opportunity for social learning (Jenkins, Antil, Wayne, & Vadasy, 2003). Effective cooperative learning structures should include the following basic elements: (a) a common task, (b) small-group learning, (c) positive interdependence, (d) individual accountability, and (e) evaluation of group work (Murphy, Grey, & Honan, 2005; Prater, 2007) Cooperative learning structures vary in complexity and level of implementation difficulty. Table 2.10 includes a list of cooperative learning structures that are commonly implemented.

The cooperative learning structures listed in Table 2.10 can be implemented to enhance academic learning in various content areas (e.g., reading, math, social studies, and science). Not only do students benefit academically when they work in cooperative learning groups, but they can also benefit socially. Social skills are utilized when students engage in cooperative learning activities. Students develop and use interpersonal skills

TABLE 2.10   Cooperative Learning Structures

COOPERATIVE DESCRIPTION	LEARNING STRUCTURE
Think-Pair-Share	Partners answer questions separately, discuss their answers together, and then share their responses with the class.
Learning Together	Learning together is not tied to specific curriculum or subjects, the structure involves five elements: positive interdependence, individual accountability, face-to-face interaction, cooperative skill training, and group processing.
Teams-Games-Tournaments	Teams study in heterogeneous groups to master learning, and then students individually apply learning as homogeneous groups play competitive games.
Jigsaw	Each member of the cooperative group becomes an expert on a specific aspect of one topic of study. After becoming an expert, teammates teach one another.
Group Investigation	With group investigation, students plan and carry out a course of study for a specific topic or unit.

Sources: Goodwin, 1999; Murphy, Grey, & Honan, 2005.

as they communicate, build effective working relationships, lead one another, manage conflict, and solve problems.

Like cooperative learning, peer-mediated instruction is a form of engaged social learning. With peer-mediated instruction, students serve as instructional assistants for classmates and/or other children (Maheady, Harper, & Mallette, 2001). The term peer implies that the students involved are the same general age or grade level. When implemented in classrooms, teachers plan instruction and train students how to tutor one another. Tutoring structures can be reciprocal, meaning the two students involved switch roles and responsibilities, and nonreciprocal, in which students do not switch roles (Prater, 2007). As with cooperative learning structures, social skills are necessary for developing effective peer-tutoring relationships.

Possible Difficulties Working with Others

As discussed in Part I, students with disabilities often experience difficulty interacting socially. Although research indicates that they can benefit academically and socially when included in cooperative learning groups and when they participate in peer-mediated instruction (Murphy et al., 2005; Prater, 2007); including students with disabilities, in both forms of social-learning structures can be problematic. Some students with disabilities may lack the academic skills necessary for making meaningful contributions to group learning. Other students may be withdrawn or disruptive. They may refuse to actively contribute to group learning, or the stress of group interactions may cause the students to behave inappropriately (e.g., yelling or leaving the group). Also, it may be difficult for some students to transition from individual work to group/peer work.

Accommodations and Adaptations that Address Difficulty Working with Others

For these reasons, it is important to provide support that enables students with disabilities to experience success in working in cooperative learning groups or with peers. Described below are suggested accommodations and adaptations that address problems in working with peers.

Carefully Select Suitable Work Partners or Groups for Students with Mild to Moderate Disabilities.   Assign students who exhibit withdrawn behavior to work with students who are supportive. Disruptive students should not be assigned to work with students who set them off or aggravate their behavior. In some cases, it may be necessary to reduce the number of students in a group and to assign a student with disruptive behavior to work with only one partner (Prater, 2007).

Explicitly Teach Tutoring or Cooperative Learning Procedures.   Before letting students tutor or work in cooperative learning groups, teach them the tutoring or cooperative learning procedures. Provide explicit step-by-step instructions for implementing elements of the selected structure (Murphy et. al., 2005). For example, if students are assigned to work in dyads to study sight words, teach them how to study the words together (see Figure 2.14).

Teach Students Cooperative Learning Social Skills.   Students use many social skills when they work together. Observe the students in your class and determine which skills need to be taught for specific structures. Table 2.11 provides a list of skills you can teach.

Teach Students Skills Necessary for Functioning Effectively as a Group.   Four levels of group functioning include forming, functioning, formulating, and fermenting (Goodwin, 1999). Forming skills are those needed to organize the group and to establish boundaries for group behavior such as moving into groups and giving directions. Functioning skills are skills necessary for managing the group's activities—expressing support, providing constructive feedback, and extending a member's answers. Formulating involves interacting in ways that facilitate deep levels of understanding, such as asking questions and discussing concepts. Fermenting skills are skills used when students draw conclusions and synthesize learning to write final reports (Goodwin, 1999). Skills associated with each of these levels can be taught to support cooperative learning activities.

When teaching cooperative learning skills, use effective teaching practices: (a) name the skill to be learned, (b) explain the skill and describe when to use it, (c) allow students to practice the skill, (d) provide feedback and correction as necessary, and (e) encourage mastery (Goodwin, 1999).

Student A: Show your partner the first sight word. If the student correctly reads the word, mark correct and show your partner the next word. Continue showing your partner words until your partner reads all 30 words.

Handling errors: If your partner does not read a word correctly, tell your partner the word and then ask your partner to read it again. Mark the word as incorrect and put the word back in the pile with the other unread sight words. The second time your partner reads the word, mark if the word was read correctly. If the word was read incorrectly the second time, put the word in the needs more study pile.

Marking responses: For each word your partner reads correctly, put a check mark in the box. For each incorrect response, put a zero in the box.

Student B: It is your turn to show words. Repeat the procedures described for Student A.

Data Collection Sheet

Words	Correct/Incorrect	Correct/Incorrect Second Time Shown
there	✓	
our	✓	
were	✓	
that	0	✓

FIGURE 2.14   Tutoring Procedures.

Suggestions for Culturally or Linguistically Diverse Students

When in a large group, humans are generally attracted to individuals who are similar to themselves. Students in classrooms are no different. So if there are two or more students from, for example, the same ethnic group, they usually gravitate toward one another in the lunchroom, on the playground, or in self-selected small-group activities. This is natural and should not be discouraged. However, there are also times in which teachers should assign small-group membership. Cooperative learning can help ELLs because it "can provide more time to practice English with a focus on negotiating meaning rather than just talking about the weather" (Farrell, 2006, p. 33).

Use Heterogeneity when Assigning Students to Work in Small Groups.   That is, mix students with various attributes (e.g., gender, ability, ethnicity) within the group. Mixing students is usually encouraged when assigning work in groups given that students naturally form homogeneous groups at other times. The more opportunities students have to interact with students who are different from themselves, the better.

TABLE 2.11   Social Skills Instruction

SOCIAL BEHAVIOR	SPECIFIC SKILL
Conversation Skills	Beginning a conversation
	Ending a conversation
Listening Skills	Active listening
	Listening and questioning techniques
Perspective Taking	Recognizing others feelings
	Showing understanding of feelings
	Expressing concern for others
	Understanding teasing
Predicting Consequences	Avoiding trouble
	Staying out of fights
	Problem solving
	Accepting consequences

Source: From "We Are Social Beings: Learning How to Learn Cooperatively" by D. M. Gut, *TEACHING Exceptional Children, 32*, 2000, 46–55. Copyright 2000 by the Council for Exceptional Children. Reprinted with permission.

Keep Group Size Limited to Three to Four Students so that All Students Feel They Can Make a Contribution.   If groups become too large, students who are ELLs or students who lack confidence speaking with their peers may allow others to dominate and may not make contributions. With only three or four students per group, it is more difficult for students to withdraw.

Encourage Everyone to Participate.   Use "talking chips" to encourage all students to participate in cooperative learning activities. Give students "talking chips." Talking chips are tokens students can use to indicate they have participated in their group activity. When a group member makes a comment, the student who made the comment places his or her chip in the middle of the table. No one in the group is allowed to add a second chip to the table until everyone in the group has added one chip (Hadaway et al., 2004). This ensures that all group members are given an opportunity to contribute to the activity.

Play Paraphrasing Passport to Give Students Extra Practice Using Their Language Skills.   Cooperative learning activities provide opportunity for students to interact with peers and to use emerging language skills. When grouping students, mix ELLs with students who are proficient in speaking and understanding English (Zehler, 1994). As students discuss ideas, have students paraphrase a previously shared idea before making comments or introducing new ideas (Hadaway et al., 2004). This enhances comprehension and allows students to repeat words and phrases they hear other students using.

■ ■ ■ ■ ■

ASSESSING LEARNING

Imagine if you were asked to complete a fourth-grade mathematical word problem test. You know you have mastered the skills of setting up the proper mathematical problem and computing accurately. However, when you go to take the test, the word problems are in Mandarin Chinese, a language you cannot read. The manner in which this test has been designed is inhibiting your ability to show your mastery of fourth-grade math.

Then suppose you are on your way to take a driver's license exam when you drop and step on your eyeglasses. Because your vision is poor, you know you will fail the driving test. In fact, it would not be safe to place you behind the wheel! Although the purpose of the driving test is to determine whether you can drive competently, without your glasses you will not be able to demonstrate how well you can drive.

These two examples are not unlike how assessment tools can inhibit students' abilities to demonstrate what they know or what they can do. In the first example, you are competent in completing fourth-grade word problems, but the language in which they are written hampers your ability to do well or anything at all. In the second example, you need your eyeglasses, an accommodation, to show the examiner you can drive a car. Allowing you to use your glasses while taking the test does not change the content or the nature of the test. The same can be said about providing test accommodations for students with disabilities. Accommodations are designed to provide access to, not change the content of, the test.

Assessment is "the process of using any tool or technique to measure student performance and behavior to make educational decisions" (Prater, 2007, p. 159). Teachers use assessment tools every day for purposes such as determining what students know, where to place students in the curriculum, or what grades to assign.

POSSIBLE DIFFICULTIES TAKING ASSESSMENTS

All the potential problems students with disabilities may exhibit discussed in Part I can impact their ability to perform on assessments. Obvious difficulties arise if students have difficulty in remembering information or staying attentive for long periods of time. Lack of motivation to do well can also greatly impact their performance on assessments. Students who are slow at processing information may not complete a test on time, or those with reading difficulties may misread the test directions.

TYPES OF ASSESSMENT

Although assessment may be categorized across many dimensions, we classify them for purposes of this section into two categories: curriculum-based assessment and high-stakes testing. Both categories are used by teachers and impact students with mild to moderate disabilities.

Curriculum-Based Assessment

Curriculum-based assessment (CBA) refers to the tools teachers use in their class-rooms to make instructional decisions. These assessments should be aligned with the learning outcomes, which in turn should be aligned with the curriculum or the content being taught. Students with disabilities may need accommodations for CBA. For each type of assessment administered, teachers decide which accommodations are appropriate based on the subject, nature of the assessment, and the knowledge or skill being assessed (Prater, 2007).

CBA can take many forms. We have divided them into three categories: (a) observations, (b) permanent products, and (c) written tests. Each is briefly described below.

Observations.   CBAs that are based on observations involve teachers watching students perform or behave. These observations may take place in naturally occurring settings or the student may be asked to perform a skill. For example, suppose you were interested in how well students serve a volleyball. A naturally occurring way to observe this would be to have the class play a volleyball game during Physical Education. A less natural way would be to line students up and ask them to serve the ball one by one. Observing in natural settings is, however, often difficult to do and thus teachers often create situations that allow them to observe students. Other CBA observation examples include watching as students present an oral report, recite a speech, perform a scientific experiment, respond orally to specific questions, and interact with peers.

How teachers collect the assessment data for observations vary greatly and are dependent on the type of observation. In the example of serving a volleyball, you could create a checklist of the elements of an effective serve and then either check off (e.g., observed or not observed) or rate (e.g., one to four) the elements observed. Table 3.1 provides an example of a checklist for oral reports, and Table 3.2 is a checklist for observing classroom behavior. Rubrics (described later under the permanent products discussion) can also be used when observing students.

Permanent Products, Rubrics, and Portfolios.   The second general type of CBA is permanent products. Permanent products include such items as essay papers, worksheets,

TABLE 3.1 Checklist for Grading Oral Reports

ORAL REPORT CHECKLIST	RATING
Opening Introduced topic and previewed main points	0 Did not include an opening 1 Introduced the topic but did not preview main points 2 Introduced the topic and previewed main points
Body Main points discussed	0 Discussed one main point 1 Discussed two main points 2 Discussed three main points
Closing Summary of the main ideas	0 Did not include a summary 1 Summarized one or two main points 2 Summarized three main points
Content Visuals	0 Did not include visual representations 1 Included one visual representation 2 Included two visual representations
Time Length of the presentation	0 Presentation was less than four minutes 1 Presentation exceeded five minutes 2 Presentation was four to five minutes
Presentation Style Eye contact	0 Did not look at the audience 1 Looked at the audience for part of the presentation 2 Maintained eye contact for the entire presentation
Comments:	Total points for presentation

art projects, portfolios, and so forth. Permanent products have an advantage over observations in that the assessment does not need to take place as the student performs the skill. A permanent product can be evaluated any time after it is completed because it is, after all, permanent.

The manner in which you assess permanent products depends on the product. Checklists, rating scales, or rubrics could be used. Rubrics provide guidelines for measuring achievement by describing the learning outcomes and performance criteria. They usually include a rating scale or checklist for evaluating the performance and descriptors to serve as examples (Venn, 2007). An example of a rubric for written papers is provided in Figure 3.1.

TABLE 3.2   Checklist for Observing Classroom Behavior

BEHAVIOR	EXHIBITED BEHAVIOR	
	😊 YES	☹ NO
Hands to self	😊	☹
Feet to self	😊	☹
Stay with the group	😊	☹
Follow directions	😊	☹

	RATING = 3	RATING = 2	RATING = 1
Level of Understanding	High level. Demonstrates ability to evaluate, synthesize, and compare and contrast ideas.	Moderate level. Demonstrates ability to compare and contrast ideas.	Low level. Presents ideas without comparing and contrasting them.
Thoroughness	At least five main ideas are addressed and three details are explained for each.	Three to four main ideas are addressed with one to three details for each.	One to two main ideas are addressed with one to three details for each.
Accuracy	All main ideas and details are accurate.	All main ideas are accurate. Includes one incorrect detail.	All main ideas are accurate. Includes more than one incorrect detail.
Writing	Well organized. Logic easy to follow. Includes an introduction, body, and conclusion.	Generally organized. Logic generally easy to follow. Includes a body with at least an introduction or conclusion.	Somewhat organized. Logic not always easy to follow. Includes a body, but no introduction or conclusion.
Mechanics	No grammatical or spelling errors.	No more than two grammatical or spelling errors.	More than two grammatical or spelling errors.

FIGURE 3.1   Rubric Example for a Written Paper.

In addition to checklists, rating scales, or rubrics, teachers often calculate "points" or percent correct with permanent products. Sometimes teachers simply assign a letter grade. The key is to ensure that the criteria used to judge the accuracy, completeness, and quality of a permanent product is clear to both you and your students.

A special form of permanent product is a portfolio. Portfolios are a purposeful collection of authentic samples of student work. "Most portfolios include evidence of student reflection and self-evaluation, guidelines for selecting the portfolio contents, and criteria for judging the quality of the work" (Venn, 2007, pp. 444–445). Portfolios can be classified as either process or product portfolios. The process portfolio documents improved learning over time. A writing sample from the beginning of the year and a second one from the end of the year could be used to document the student's growth during the year. The product portfolio, on the other hand, focuses on demonstrating mastery and would include only the final paper.

Written Tests.   Written tests are the last general type of CBA. Although tests can also be oral or performance based, in this context we are referring to paper-pencil tests that students take to demonstrate their knowledge of particular information being or having been taught. Most people think about tests being administered after the instruction has occurred. This is called summative assessment. In contrast, formative assessment is administered frequently and while learning is still occurring (Prater, 2007). Formative assessment allows you to evaluate not only your students' progress but your teaching as well. If students aren't learning, you can adjust your instruction. Unfortunately, teachers often use only summative assessment (e.g., end-of-unit test, midterm exams), and regardless of student performance on that assessment, teachers move on to teaching new content. Most assessment that takes place in the classroom is testing, and many, if not most of those tests require that students read directions and questions and respond in writing. Written tests are used primarily for the convenience of the teacher. It is easier to administer a written test individually or as a group than to orally quiz each student on his or her knowledge. Yet, written tests are usually the most difficult for students with disabilities to complete.

CBA can be as flexible as is the teacher. Because CBA hasn't been standardized to require prescribed administration procedures, appropriate test accommodations can be made more easily than when using standardized tests.

Using Curriculum-Based Assessment

Below we describe ways in which teachers can make accommodations for CBAs. Additional suggestions provided later in this section also apply to CBAs.

Consider Using Oral Responses for Some Students.   Given that students with disabilities often have difficulty reading and writing, they may better demonstrate their knowledge of the content in other ways, such as through oral reports, oral presentations, or oral responses to questions.

Use Cross-Grade Evaluators, Other School Personnel, and/or Volunteers to Help Observe or Grade.   If you determine that oral responses are more appropriate than written ones, include other people to help you observe or grade student performance. Older students, school personnel such as paraeducators, volunteers in the classroom, or university students can be trained to be observers for assessment purposes. These individuals can also help assess permanent products and written tests.

Provide Explicit Directions Orally and in Writing.   Regardless of the type of assessment being used, be certain to provide clear instructions on what students are expected to do. Directions should be given orally as well as in writing. Students with disabilities may not understand the directions if given only once. One advantage of using CBA over high-stakes testing is that the administration procedures are not standardized. Thus, reading the directions to the students will not change how you interpret their performance on the test. After reading the directions, ask students to repeat back what they heard and ensure they have no questions before administering the test.

Provide Students with a Copy of the Assessment Tool (e.g., rubric, checklist) in Advance. Explain the Criteria to Students.   All students, but particularly those with disabilities, benefit from knowing in advance how they will be evaluated. By providing copies of assessment tools and explaining grading criteria, students can better prepare for tests. In addition, there will be fewer disagreements after a test has been graded about the criteria used for assigning grades.

Allow More Time for Students to Take a Written Test if They Need It.   Unless it is a timed test, allow students more time to complete the test. Some students with disabilities process information slower and, if given sufficient time to complete a test, will be able to better demonstrate what they know and can do.

Break the Administration of a Longer Test into Smaller Time Periods.   Some students perform best when they are asked to concentrate for smaller periods of time. If this is the case, break the test into sections in advance and administer the sections one at a time.

Test Smaller Chunks of Information More Frequently.   Often, particularly at the secondary level, students take exams that cover a large domain of information. This can be hard for students with disabilities because they have difficulty with long-term memory and short attention spans. Rather than using an end-of-unit approach to testing, break the information into smaller pieces. For example, a history unit may be the Revolutionary War. Instead of waiting until all information about the Revolutionary War is taught and then giving a unit test at the end of the month, break the content into week-long units and administer one test each Friday.

High-Stakes Testing

In contrast to CBA, large-scale assessments are used to assess whether all students have met district or state standards. These data are used primarily for the purpose of accountability and have been labeled "high-stakes" because of the serious consequences if students do not pass them (Council for Exceptional Children, 2001). Some states use them to determine if students can advance to the next grade level or graduate.

The Individuals with Disabilities Education Act (IDEA) requires that students with disabilities be included in high-stakes testing with accommodations in administration, if necessary. Each student's individualized education program (IEP) team determines the extent to which high-stakes testing is appropriate for the individual student. The IEP team also determines what accommodations, if needed, would be appropriate.

High-stakes tests are generally standardized tests and must be administered using prespecified procedures. Any changes in these procedures can influence the interpretation of test scores. However, without accommodations, students with disabilities may not demonstrate their full potential, and their test scores underrepresent what they know and can do. Most publishers of standardized tests provide a list of testing accommodations appropriate for specific tests.

IMPROVING STUDENTS' TEST-TAKING SKILLS

All students could benefit from being taught test-taking strategies. Such strategies can help them with both CBA and high-stakes tests. Those who demonstrate effective test-taking strategies are considered *testwise*. For example, suppose two students with equal knowledge of the content being tested enter the testing situation at the same time. Student 1 knows how to use time wisely, eliminate obviously incorrect choices on multiple-choice tests, and review answers before submitting the test. Student 2 does not have these skills. Which student will answer more items correctly? The testwise student will perform better, not because he knows the content better, but because he knows and can apply appropriate test-taking strategies. Teachers must remember that being testwise, however, isn't sufficient for students to perform well on tests. They also need to know the content.

Test scores are not always reflective of what students know and can do. Many variables impact test performance. For example, a student who comes into a testing situation very hungry or very sleepy will not perform to her best ability. If something emotional is occurring in her life, such as divorce or the death of a loved one, this, too, can greatly impact test performance. Teachers need to be aware of these potential problems and do all they can to alleviate the impact on the student's performance. Below are some examples of ways teachers can help students perform well in testing situations.

Inform Students Regarding What, When, and How They Will Be Tested.   Students need to know what they will be tested on. This helps them prepare. They will also be much more prepared if they know when the test will be given. Using surprise quizzes, for example, is generally not helpful for this population and may contribute to their frustration about test taking. Explaining what types of test questions will be used (e.g., multiple choice, essay) and providing practice will also better prepare students.

TEST REMINDER

Test Date: Wednesday, February 15

Subject: Social Studies

Unit: Westward Expansion

20 Multiple Choice and 3 Short-answer Questions about the:

- Louisiana Purchase
- Lewis and Clark Expedition
- Overland Routes
- Means of Transportation (Pony express, stagecoaches, railroads, canals, and wagon trains)

2 Maps to Label

- Routes of Expansion (Oregon Trail, Cumberland Road, Sante Fe Trail, Old Spanish Trail, California Trail)
- North American Map (U.S. before 1803, Louisiana Purchase, Spanish Territory, and Disputed territory)

FIGURE 3.2   Test Reminder.

Provide Students with Reminder Notes Several Days Before the Test Will Be Administered.
Print the reminder notes on brightly colored paper to stand out in their notebooks or at home (see Figure 3.2). Include the date, as well as information on what the test will cover. In fact, all of the items mentioned earlier regarding what, when, and how they will be tested should be included.

Remind Students to Come Prepared Physically for the Assessment.   Students who come in good health—well rested and having eaten properly—perform better on tests (Scruggs & Mastropieri, 1992). If reminded several days in advance, students can have a head start in preparing physically.

Provide a Healthy, Positive, and Confident Atmosphere.   Students who have a history of poor test performance often feel discouraged and are not motivated to do well. Help students set realistic goals for themselves and provide a supportive environment, even when the student doesn't perform well (Scruggs & Mastropieri, 1992b).

Provide Practice Tests Using the Format of the Actual Test with Items that Closely Align with the Questions Students Will Encounter.   If students are used to the format of the test and the types of test questions, they can focus their energy on answering the question, and not on trying to discern the type of problems being asked.

Teach Relaxation and Adrenalin–Reducing Techniques.   Students need to feel as relaxed as possible during a testing situation. A common relaxation technique is to take deep breaths through your nose and exhale through your mouth. Also, extra adrenalin can be disposed of through physical activity. Have students run, for example, once around the school building or do a series of jumping jacks right before the test is administered.

Provide External Reinforcement for Effort.   Students should be reinforced not only for how well they did but also for how well they tried. This can be done by providing partial credit for attempted items and/or by giving reinforcers for staying on task during the test administration.

Teach Students to Attribute Success/Failure to Personal Effort and Not to Forces Outside the Students' Control.   Students who have a history of poor school performance often attribute their failures to internal but stable causes ("I am dumb and I will always be dumb."), and they attribute their successes to external factors ("I did well because it was my lucky day."). These individuals can be taught to connect task success or failure with their effort and application of skills and knowledge (Kozminsky & Kozminsky, 2002).

Teach Students General Test-Taking Strategies that Can Apply to Many Different Tests.   That is, teach procedures that students can complete while preparing for or taking a test. For example, acronyms have been developed to help students remember strategy steps for taking tests. These procedures can be taught using teacher-directed instruction as described in Part I. For example, the acronym FORCE can be taught to students to help them prepare for tests. *F* stands for find out about the test, *O* for organize, *R* for review, *C* for concentrate, and *E* for early exam (practice) (Wehrung-Schaffner & Sapona, 1990). This example and three others may be found in Table 3.3. A sample lesson plan of the SCORER strategy is in Appendix A.

Teach Students Strategies that are Specific to the Type of Question Being Asked.   Different types of questions require different strategies. Successful multiple-choice test takers know how to eliminate the obvious and less obvious wrong answers to deduce the correct response. Those who do well with essay items know how to organize their thoughts and express those thoughts in writing. Table 3.4 outlines the strategies that are appropriate for multiple-choice, sentence completion, and essay questions.

Teach Students Strategies Specific to High-Stakes Testing.   The format for high-stakes tests is often different than other tests students take. For example, the separate answer sheet with bubbles that are filled in can be difficult for a student who makes mistakes tracking from the test question sheet to the answer sheet. Table 3.5 describes high-stakes test-taking strategies that students can be taught. Several of the strategies apply to other types of tests as well.

Accommodations and Adaptations for All Types of Assessments

Test accommodations are defined as changes made in the way the test is administered. Test modifications, on the other hand, refer to changes in the content of the test (Elliott, McKevitt, & Kettler, 2002). Accommodations do not come one size fits all.

TABLE 3.3   Examples of Test-Taking Strategies

Test Preparation	**FORCE** (Wehrung-Schaffner & Sapona, 1990)
	Find out (what the test will cover and what types of questions will be asked).
	Organize (by collecting all the necessary materials to study).
	Review the material.
	Concentrate and make a cue sheet.
	Early exam (practice by drilling or having a partner ask you questions).
During the Test	**PIRATES** (Hughes & Schumaker, 1991)
	Prepare to succeed.
	Inspect the instructions.
	Read, remember, reduce.
	Answer or abandon.
	Turn back.
	Estimate.
	Survey.
	SCORER (Carman & Adams, 1984)
	Schedule time.
	Clue words, look for.
	Omit difficult questions.
	Read carefully.
	Estimate answers.
	Review your work.
	SNOW (Scruggs & Mastropieri, 1992)
	Study the question.
	Note important points.
	Organize important information before writing.
	Write directly to the point of the question.

Source: Teaching Strategies for Students with Mild to Moderate Disabilities by M. A. Prater, 2007, Boston: Allyn & Bacon. Reprinted with permission.

They should be based on the student's individual strengths and limitations. Below we describe ways in which accommodations can be made so that students with disabilities can demonstrate what they know and can do.

Make Adjustments in the Testing Setting.   The testing setting refers to changing the conditions or location of the testing situation. For example, rather than completing a test in a large group, students could be placed in small groups or provided with study carrels to help keep them focused and less distracted. Other examples include administering the

TABLE 3.4   Test-Taking Strategies Categorized by Type of Test Item

TEST ITEM TYPES	TEST-TAKING STRATEGIES
Multiple Choice	■ Before reading the choices, try to answer the question. ■ Consider all choices carefully. ■ Eliminate choices. ■ Look for clue words (statements like *always* or *rarely*). ■ Compare the choices with each other and the relationship to the step statements.
Sentence Completion	■ If unsure of the answer, guess. ■ Fill in at least partial information. ■ Make the sentence consistent and logical.
Essay	■ Answer every item. ■ Use your time wisely. ■ If writing your answers, use your best penmanship.

Source: Teaching Strategies for Students with Mild to Moderate Disabilities by M. A. Prater, 2007, Boston: Allyn & Bacon. Reprinted with permission.

test individually or in a separate room, moving the test-taker's location in the room, or providing adaptive furniture (Thurlow, Elliott, & Ysseldyke, 2003).

Change the Duration or Organization of the Testing Time.   Students who use adaptive equipment (e.g., Brailler, CD player with earphones, magnification equipment) may need additional time. Students who process information slowly may also need additional time. Providing additional time to complete the test is one of the most frequently requested accommodations but should be used only if students truly need more time to help compensate for their disability (Thurlow et al., 2003). Other examples include allowing the student to take frequent breaks and scheduling short testing segments.

Adjust When the Test is Administered.   When the test is given can impact students' performance. Students with attention deficits or physical disabilities may need to have a long test broken up into smaller parts and administered across multiple times, and even multiple days. Adjustments can also be made in terms of the time of the day the test is administered. Students on medication, for example, may have particularly good times of the day due to the effects of their medication.

Alter the Format of the Test or How it is Administered.   Format alterations are changes that are made on the test itself and include such alterations as fewer number of items per page, large-print version of the test, key words highlighted, and cues (e.g., arrows) on the answer form. Examples of changing the test administration include reading directions to the student, providing additional examples, prompting the student to stay

TABLE 3.5 Test–Taking Strategies for High-Stakes Tests

STRATEGY	OBJECTIVES
Bubble sheet completion and timing	Fill in bubbles completely. Be aware of how much available time is remaining. Pace yourself when taking a test. Answer all problems before time expires.
Sorting problems	Sort problems by differentiating between easier and more difficult problems. Complete the easy problems prior to attempting the more difficult ones. Sort problems based on similarity in content.
Estimation	Estimate answers in math problems by using rounding.
Substitution and backsolving	Substitute the answers provided on a multiple-choice test into the question being asked to find the one correct answer.
Recopying problems	Rewrite problems in a more familiar form to make them easier to solve.
Underlining and reading all answers	Identify exactly what the question is asking you to do. Read all questions carefully to make better answer choices. Underline key words and phrases in the question.
Elimination	Eliminate absurd multiple-choice answers. Eliminate answers with redundant or similar information. Eliminate answers with extreme qualifiers.

Source: "Preparing Adolescents with High-incidence Disabilities for High-stakes Testing with Strategy Instruction" by E. W. Carter, J. Wehby, C. Hughes, S. M. Johnson, D. R. Plank, S. M. Barton-Arwood, & L. B. Lunsford, *Preventing School Failure, 49* (2), 2005, 55–62. Reprinted with permission.

focused, clarifying or explaining the directions, and answering questions about items without giving the answer.

Provide Assistive Devices. Assistive devices can accommodate both how the test is presented as well as how the student responds. For example, accommodations such as audio taping the directions, using a template to reduce visual print, applying pencil grips, or using magnets/tape to secure papers to the desk are all ways of using assistive devices for test presentation. Using assistive devices for student responding include allowing students to use a Brailler, word processor, computer, calculator, spell checker, and so forth.

Use Format Alterations.   Examples of format alterations include allowing the students to mark their responses on the test rather than a separate page or on a different type of paper, such as graph paper.

Change Testing Procedures.   Procedure changes include allowing students to use reference materials or give their response in a different way (e.g., point to the answer, oral not written response) (Bolt & Thurlow, 2004).

Always Select Accommodations that Are the Least Intrusive.   Some accommodations take more time and effort than others for the person administering the test (e.g., the teacher) and/or the student. Always use the accommodations that are easiest to implement and that are still appropriate for the student. For example, if a student has difficulty handwriting responses but can use a word processor, the word processor would be less intrusive than a scribe (Bolt & Thurlow, 2004).

Train Those Who are Administering the Accommodations.   Any person who is assisting with accommodations, whether it is a classmate, a paraeducator, or a volunteer, needs to be trained. For example, those who act as scribes need prior instruction to only write down verbatim responses. Readers may need instructions to only read the directions and not provide an explanation (Bolt & Thurlow, 2004).

Before Testing, Make Certain You Know Exactly What Skills You are Intending to Measure to Ensure Accommodations Do Not Interfere.   For example, if the intent of a writing test is to measure how well students can express themselves, using a word processor or a scribe would be appropriate. If, on the other hand, the intent of a writing test is to measure handwriting, a word processor or scribe would not be appropriate (Bolt & Thurlow, 2004).

Make Sure Students Have Used the Testing Accommodations During Instruction as Well.   The accommodations provided during the testing situation should not be the first time the student has used the accommodation. Accommodations appropriate for testing are also appropriate for instruction. In fact, there should be a direct link between accommodations provided in both settings (Bolt & Thurlow, 2004).

Suggestions for Culturally or Linguistically Diverse Students

Students from cultural or linguistically different backgrounds may experience additional difficulty with test taking. As described at the beginning of this section, language plays a huge role in assessment. Whether students need to read or listen to directions, if they do not understand the language they will not perform well. Experiential backgrounds and prior knowledge also affects the test performance of this population. For example, in history, *out west* refers to the unsettled U.S. Western frontier. Many children learn this by reading, watching television, or listening to conversations of adults. But children of poverty, immigrants, or ELLs most likely would not have been exposed to this concept outside school. In fact, the term *west* implies west of the east coast of the U.S. mainland. Immigrants who came from Asian countries were not settling out west, but rather *out east* from their previous homeland.

Students new to the U.S. school system will experience differences from their previous schooling, which includes assessment expectations. To level the playing field, these students must be explicitly taught their school's assessment culture. "Great differences will be apparent in study skills, mechanics of testing, the definition of plagiarism, the morality of doing group work when individual work is expected [and so forth]" (Ariza, 2006, p. 146).

Explicitly Teach Students When it Is and Is Not Appropriate to Share Work. In many countries and cultural groups, group work is the norm and sharing someone else's work is not wrong. Students need to be taught when it is okay to share work (and other things) and when it is not. Once students understand these concepts, they can be held accountable for their actions.

When Appropriate, Use Authentic Assessment. Authentic assessment refers to products and other types of assessment tools that are close to expectations in the real world. These are the preferred methods of measuring achievement for ELLs (Ariza, 2006). Examples of authentic assessment include drawings, projects, charts, concept maps, audio or videotapes, and so forth.

Don't Assume Students Understand the Format of the Test. For example, immigrant students who are used to taking essay exams in their native country schools may not know how to use a separate answer sheet with little bubbles (Ariza, 2006).

Allow ELLs to Use Dictionaries, Both English and Primary Language to English. The use of the dictionaries will take extra time. Thus, consider providing extended testing time beyond the amount given to others or specified in the testing manual to compensate for this additional time.

GRADING ADAPTATIONS

Teaching test-taking skills and providing assessment accommodations can improve students with disabilities' test performance. However, classroom grades usually represent more than test performance. Other assessments are also factored into grades, and students with disabilities have increased risk for receiving low, inaccurate grades that lack meaning in terms of academic progress (Silva, Munk, & Bursuck, 2005). Depending on classroom circumstances and students' specific disabilities, grades might not accurately report students' effort and achievement; instead, they could reflect students' disabilities (e.g., problems with organization, writing deficits, reading difficulty).

The purpose of grading is to communicate information about students' achievement, progress in the classroom curriculum, and effort-expended learning. Grades can also provide motivation for learning and are used to compare a student's performance with his or her peers (Salend & Duhaney, 2002). For students with disabilities, it is important to evaluate whether these purposes are being served. Students who consistently receive low or failing grades can easily become discouraged, particularly if they do not feel they have control over their grades. Adapting grading practices is one way to help them become more involved with their learning. Grading adaptations can motivate students to try harder if they have become discouraged, help them see to their progress, focus their effort on learning critical content, and teach them that work influences outcomes (Silva et al., 2005).

Teachers can legally modify grading procedures for students who have IEPs. However, it is not appropriate to modify grading procedures for students without IEPs unless such modifications are available to all students in the class (Salend & Duhaney, 2002). Most schools or school districts have grading policies, and you should review these policies prior to adapting classroom grades.

If you determine that grading adaptations are appropriate for a student who has an IEP, adaptations should focus on the needs of the student, and systematic procedures should be implemented to insure consistency. Strive to obtain consensus for grading procedures among teachers who grade the student's work and communicate your grading policies to the parents and to the student. Specific grading adaptations are discussed below.

Provide an Alternate to a Number or Letter Grade.   Instead of assigning a numeric or letter grade, mark whether students pass or fail a course or assignment (Salend & Duhaney, 2002). A pass/fail system emphasizes mastery. Minimum course competencies should be identified and specified so that students know what is required to receive a passing grade.

Use Checklists or Rating Scales to Report Mastery of Course Benchmarks.   To develop course checklists or rating scales, identify benchmarks or essential knowledge and skills. When marking students' progress, you can indicate whether skills are mastered, developing, or not yet evident (Salend & Duhaney, 2002).

Adapt Grades to Reflect Progress Meeting IEP Goals.   Part or all of students' grades can be based on meeting IEP goals (Silva et al., 2005). IEP goals identify areas targeted for improvement, and grades can reflect whether students have improved to the degree specified. For example, if an IEP goal states that a student will write a five-sentence paragraph using standard writing conventions (i.e., capital letters, proper spelling, correct sentence construction, and punctuation), part or all of a student's grade could be based on meeting this goal.

Base Part of a Student's Grade on Improved Performance.   Daily grades and final grades communicate performance, including improved performance (Salend & Duhaney, 2002). Consider basing all or part of an assignment grade on improvement over past assignments. Awarding bonus points is one way to acknowledge improvement. If a student is learning cursive and prints assignments instead of writing them, award bonus point for assignments partially or completely written in cursive. Final grades can also reflect improved performance (Silva et al., 2005). Extra points can be added to point totals if students meet specified criteria for improvement.

Add Written Comments to Report Cards.   Sometimes, grades can be confusing to parents. A parent may have a conversation with a teacher who reports that his or her child is improving in school. And yet, when the parent receives the child's report card, the parent is shocked to see low or failing grades. Adding comments to report cards is one way to clarify grading criteria and to address possible misunderstandings (e.g., "Although Ally is progressing, her achievement is still not at grade level in math."). Additionally, teachers can add comments that provide students and parents with information about students' learning styles, use of learning strategies, special talents and needs, effort, attitudes, and behavior (Salend, 2005).

Adjust the Grade Weights.   Teachers can adjust how grades are weighted when calculating final grades (Munk & Bursuck, 1998). You can take into account a student's specific disability and adjust the percent of activities, tests, and products that count toward grades so that final grades more accurately reflect a student's performance and not his or her disability.

Design a Grading System that Emphasizes Process and Effort.   "Grading systems often consider (a) products of student performance, (b) processes that students use to complete their work, and (c) effort the student puts into the work" (Silva et al., 2005, p. 90). Students' grades can be adapted to emphasize process and effort. Process involves how students complete work. Students with disabilities often do not use effective learning strategies; teaching processes or strategies for completing academic tasks, and then adapting students' grades to emphasize process can encourage students to use the strategies (Silva et al., 2005). For example, writing a formula is a process for calculating the area of geometric figures. When grading a student's assignment, the teacher could assess whether the student wrote formulas before solving area problems and could add ten percent to the student's score if he or she used the process for calculating area.

Emphasizing effort is just as important as emphasizing process. Often, students with disabilities attribute their success or failure to factors beyond their control. Adapting grades to acknowledge effort is one way to help students learn that effort influences results. When making decisions about measuring effort, teachers should involve students and parents, if possible. Points for assignments can reflect effort and performance. This can be accomplished by determining the points possible for an assignment and allotting some points for effort. If a student is given fifty points for writing a short essay, five of the fifty points could represent effort (how many paragraphs the student wrote). The teacher could specify that the student would need to write at least two paragraphs to receive the five effort points.

Prioritize Content and Base All or Part of a Student's Grade on Completing Assignments for Content Priorities.   As discussed in Part II, Accessing General Education Curriculum, teachers determine what they teach in their classrooms. As teachers review course curriculum, they decide which learning objectives are priorities and allocate time and focus accordingly. For students with disabilities, teachers can prioritize curriculum objectives and base students' grades on assignments related to critical content. For example, if a teacher plans to cover two science units during a marking period and determines that one unit is more important than the other, the teacher can prioritize assignments and have students with disabilities spend more time completing assignments for the important unit (Silva et al., 2005). This practice allows the students to work independently and to focus time and effort learning critical content. All or part of the students' grades could then be based on prioritized assignments.

PART IV

CONTENT AREA ACCOMMODATIONS

Imagine that you are on a train in a foreign country. You are enjoying your ride through the countryside when suddenly the train makes an unexpected stop. The announcer says something over the train's speaker system. Unfortunately, the announcer is speaking in a language you do not understand. You don't know what is going on, and you can't figure out what to do, if anything. To make matters worse, you notice that many of your fellow passengers are getting off your train and are rushing to board another stopped train. As you watch the other passengers get on the second train you begin to feel anxious. You don't know if you should follow them or stay on your train.

As luck would have it, an English-speaking passenger stops in your section and explains that there is an accident on the tracks and your train will be delayed until the accident is cleared—probably for one to two hours. You learn that the train the other passengers are boarding is going to the same destination as your train, but it is an express train and will not make stops along the way. When you finally understand the situation, you relax and wait for your train to continue its journey. You feel grateful that someone happened along who helped you understand the situation.

The situation described above produced anxiety because you did not speak the foreign language. Your anxiety was directly related to your language deficits. Just as you would feel anxious being in a situation in which you did not understand what was happening or being said, students with disabilities can feel anxiety when they lack skills to understand classroom instruction. Often, students with disabilities have deficits that impact their performance in specific subjects or content areas. Some students with disabilities may have math or reading and writing disabilities; others may have reasoning deficits that impact achievement in social studies, health, science, and other content area subjects. A disability in one subject, such as reading, often influences performance in other academic subjects. In such cases, students need accommodations that address their challenges in learning content area curriculum.

In this section we present accommodations for reading, writing, math, science, and social studies that enable students to acquire skills in these areas. Suggestions that apply across content areas may also be found in Part II. Considering how important basic skills are for school success and for functioning in society, it is particularly important for teachers to provide these accommodations and adaptations.

```
┌─────────────────────────────────────────────────────┐
│                                                       │
│                    READING SKILLS                     │
│                                                       │
│  ┌─────────────────────────────────────────────────┐ │
│  │                 COMPREHENSION                     │ │
│  │             Understanding written text            │ │
│  ├─────────────────────────────────────────────────┤ │
│  │                  VOCABULARY                       │ │
│  │         Understanding the meaning of words        │ │
│  ├─────────────────────────────────────────────────┤ │
│  │                   FLUENCY                         │ │
│  │   Reading quickly and accurately with expression  │ │
│  ├─────────────────────────────────────────────────┤ │
│  │                   PHONICS                         │ │
│  │        Learning that letters represent sounds     │ │
│  ├─────────────────────────────────────────────────┤ │
│  │                  PHONEMIC                         │ │
│  │                  AWARENESS                        │ │
│  │        Perceiving the sound structure of words    │ │
│  └─────────────────────────────────────────────────┘ │
└─────────────────────────────────────────────────────┘
```

FIGURE 4.1   Skills Necessary for Learning to Read.

READING

Acquiring functional reading skills is vital for school success. All subjects require reading. Reading is a complex activity, and to become proficient readers, students must possess or acquire specific reading skills. The National Reading Panel has identified phonemic awareness (the ability to perceive the sound structure of words), phonics (letter/sound correspondences), fluency (reading quickly, accurately, and with expression), vocabulary (understanding the meaning of words), and comprehension (extracting meaning from written material) skills as necessary for learning to read (Armbruster, Lehr, & Osborn, 2003) (see Figure 4.1).

Possible Difficulties Accessing Reading Instruction

Students with mild to moderate disabilities may have specific reading disabilities. Reading disabilities are manifested as deficits in reading skills. Researchers have documented that students with reading disabilities have (a) phonemic awareness or sound processing deficits, (b) comprehension problems, or (c) both sound processing and comprehension difficulties (Catts & Hogan, 2003).

When students lack phonemic awareness, they experience significant difficulty in learning to read (Armbruster et al., 2003). Such students generally have difficulty in acquiring and processing language, which impacts their ability to learn phonics. Because they lack the ability to perceive the sound structure of words, it is difficult for them to understand and learn letter/sound correspondence. When reading, they frequently do not perceive the sound structure of words and make mistakes in decoding words. For example, if a student with reading disabilities encounters the phrase *the strange withering tree,* the student might read the phrase as *the strong white tree.* The student uses the first letters of the words as cues for reading the words, not perceiving that the sounds he produces are not the same as the sounds represented in the words.

Not all students with reading disabilities have phonemic awareness deficits. Some students with reading disabilities learn phonics and develop good decoding skills. However, they may have vocabulary and comprehension deficits that impact their ability to understand what they read. Although they accurately read printed words, they do not comprehend reading material. Comprehension difficulties can stem from language deficits. For students to understand the meaning of the sentence: *The beautiful brown colt stood inside the large spacious barn,* they need to know the meaning of beautiful, colt, spacious, and barn. Students also need language skills to process descriptive words such as beautiful, brown, inside, large, and spacious in order to comprehend the sentence.

Finally, there are students who have both sound processing and comprehension deficits. For them, reading is a difficult activity. They struggle to decode unfamiliar words and they make many errors while reading. When they do not read accurately or fluently, comprehending reading material becomes a problem.

Accommodations and Adaptations that Address Problems Accessing Reading Instruction

The National Reading Panel recommends explicit instruction in all the reading skill areas to help students become proficient readers (Armbruster et al., 2003). Accommodations and instructional adaptations that help students develop phonemic awareness, phonics knowledge, fluency, vocabulary, and comprehension skills are discussed below.

Phonemic Awareness.

Teach sound segmentation. When teaching new words, teach your students to place coins or blocks to represent sounds in words. There are two sounds in the word *at.* This word can be represented by two blocks—one block for each sound (Edelen-Smith, 1997). When students manipulate objects to represent sounds, they develop sound segmentation skills.

a   t

Use rhymes. Rhyming activities help students to develop phonemic awareness. During reading instruction, incorporate rhyming activities in lessons. Students can create fun sentences using rhyming words such as: *The fat rat sat in the hat on the mat.* You can also have your students memorize nursery rhymes (Jerger, 1996).

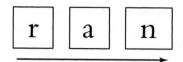

FIGURE 4.2   Prompt for Blending.

Practice manipulating sounds.   Provide opportunities for students to add or delete sounds from words. For example, by adding sounds to *at*, students can create new words such as *hat, rat, mat,* and *pat*. Taking the *s* sound off *Sam, sat,* and *pans* creates *am, at,* and *pan*.

Teach blending.   Just as students need to know how to segment sounds in words, they also need to know how to blend sounds, or put them together. Explicitly teach students how to blend sounds. This can be done by teaching students to slowly move a finger under sounds as they read each sound in a word, and then to quickly move their finger under all the sounds as they blend the sounds to read the word. Visual prompts can be used to help students learn to blend. In Figure 4.2 the word *ran* is separated into three sounds. Initially, students can touch and read each sound of the word. When they correctly read each of the three sounds, they can then be taught to run their finger along the arrow under the word as they quickly blend the three sounds together.

Phonics.

Use explicit instruction.   Use explicit, systematic methods for teaching phonics. Explicit methods involve directly teaching sounds and sound patterns. For example, when teaching students the *oi* sound, a teacher would say the following: "This sound is *oi*. Say oi." The teacher would not expect the students to discover the oi sound on their own when shown boil or foil. Frequently used letters and sounds such as *a, s,* and *t* should be taught first, and letters that are easily confused (e.g., *b* and *d*) should not be taught at the same time. Provide opportunities for students to learn letter/sound relationships in every lesson (Chard & Osborn, 1999).

Teach decoding and word analysis strategies.   After students learn sound/letter correspondences, teach strategies for decoding new words. Reading words by analogy and reading known parts of words to decode unknown parts are effective decoding strategies (Lovett, Lacarenza, Borden, Frijters, & Steinbach, 2000; Woodruff, Schumaker, & Deshler, 2002). When using analogies, students identify parts of words that are like words they already know and read the word using prior knowledge. For example, the *ain* sounds in grain are the same as sounds in rain. Students would use their knowledge of how to read rain to read the word grain.

Multisyllable words can often be divided into syllables, and students can use their knowledge of prefixes, suffixes, and word parts to read new words and to analyze word

TABLE 4.1   Word-Study Sheet Example

WORDS	WRITE THE PREFIX	WRITE THE STEM	WRITE THE SUFFIX	READ THE PARTS, READ THE WORD
pretending	*pre*	*tend*	*ing*	*pretending*
confounding	*con*	*found*	*ing*	*confounding*

structure. If students know how to read the suffix *tion,* they can isolate the suffix and read *action, nation,* and *fiction.* Provide prompt sheets that help students apply word analysis skills (see Table 4.1).

Teach students to create word banks.   Teach students how to create their own word banks, which are a student's collection of words the student can read in isolation. Have students write the words on small cards and review them frequently. Students with disabilities may forget learned words if they do not review them often (Bender & Larkin, 2003). Figure 4.3 provides an example of an emerging reader's word bank. The word bank includes sight and decodable words.

Fluency.
Teach sight words.   Sight words are decodable and nondecodable high-frequency words. Teach sight words and provide opportunities for students to practice reading the words. One method for increasing sight word fluency is to incorporate sight-word reading drills in instruction. Provide students with sight-word grids that have five words repeated a number of times on the grid (see Table 4.2). Time students as they read the words on the grid (Bender, 2002).

Use re-reading strategies.   Reading the same selection more than once helps students increase reading speed (Chard, Vaughn, & Tyler, 2002). After students have learned to read all the words in a reading selection, you can build timed readings into reading routines. Timed readings do not have to consume large amounts of instructional time. Have students open their reading selections, read for one minute, and then mark how far they have read. Then, have the students repeat the process one or two more times, encouraging them to try to read farther each time they read the selection. If students

at	mat	it	was	on
I	a	sat	or	of
is	as	car	if	and

FIGURE 4.3   Word Bank Example.

TABLE 4.2   Fluency Practice Example

HIGH-FREQUENCY WORDS: THE, IT, IS, A, ON				
the	it	is	a	on
it	the	a	on	is
is	on	the	it	a
it	the	a	on	is
is	on	the	it	a
the	it	is	a	on

become anxious being timed, you can simply give them a short passage to read and ask them to read the passage quickly and quietly two to three times.

Ensure students read accurately when building fluency.   When your students engage in fluency-building activities, make sure they can read the material accurately. Fluency is not only being able to read material quickly, but also reading correctly. Before your students practice increasing reading speed, check their accuracy. Students should only be allowed to work on reading fluency after they have demonstrated mastery of the reading selection.

Use peer tutors.   Peer tutors can serve as models of fluent reading (Mastropieri, Leinart, & Scruggs, 1999). Assign a strong reader to work with a student who is having difficulty in reading. The fluent reader models fluent reading as the partner follows along. Roles are switched and the partner reads while the fluent reader monitors and corrects reading errors. It is important that students do not practice errors, and students with disabilities may need feedback and correction to ensure they are reading accurately (Armbruster et al., 2003). Before implementing peer tutoring, students should be trained on how to provide feedback and correction. Teachers should determine error correction procedures, model how to correct errors, provide opportunities for peer tutors to practice procedures as the teacher provides feedback and correction, and then monitor tutors as they work with peers.

Vocabulary.
Pre-teach vocabulary.   Before assigning reading selections, teach students new vocabulary words. New vocabulary can be taken out of context and taught prior to reading a selection. For example, a passage about protecting criminals might contain the following new vocabulary words: landmark, lascivious, self-incrimination, and conviction. The meanings of these words can be taught before students read them in context. When teaching new words, illustrate the meaning with numerous examples, relate the words to students' prior knowledge, and provide opportunities for the students to discuss meaning and apply their knowledge.

Use pictures and objects to illustrate meaning.   For students with disabilities, visual representations can be easier to remember than words. Use pictures to illustrate meaning. For example, when teaching students that birds are warm-blooded animals, provide a

TABLE 4.3   Reading Schedule

DAY	READING SELECTION
Monday	*Fiction—Out of Africa*
Tuesday	*Fiction—Out of Africa*
Wednesday	*Nonfiction—Kilimanjaro article*
Thursday	*Nonfiction—Kilimanjaro article*
Friday	*Nonfiction—Africa current issues article*

picture of a bird basking in the sunlight. The sunny scene facilitates the understanding of the term warm blooded (Scruggs & Mastropieri, 1992a).

Use mnemonic devices.   As discussed in Part II (remembering information), mnemonic devices can be incorporated in instruction. Keyword is a mnemonic device that can be used to help students learn new vocabulary words (Uberti et al., 2003). With key-words, students learn the definition of a new word by associating the word with an image and keyword that illustrates meaning. For example, to teach *daunt,* the keyword *haunt* can be used. The meaning of daunt can be illustrated with the image of a ghost haunting and intimidating people.

Vary reading activities.   Expose students to a broad range of fiction and nonfiction material. Schedule time for students to read and to listen to a variety of books. This provides opportunities for students to build listening and reading vocabularies (Adams, 1990). Table 4.3 provides an example of a reading schedule.

Comprehension.
Use story-reading guides and graphic organizers.   Give students story-reading guides, which are guides that provide prompts for identifying important aspects of stories. Provide graphic organizers for reading selections to help students focus attention on important aspects of the selections (Armbruster et al., 2003) (see Table 4.4).

Teach comprehension strategies.   Explicitly teach comprehension strategies. Strategies proven effective for improving comprehension are the following: self-questioning, identification of main ideas, summarizing information, activating prior knowledge, actively monitoring and repairing comprehension, and bypass reading (Armbruster et al., 2003; Dyck & Pemberton, 2002).

- **Self-questioning.** Teach students to ask themselves questions as they read so that they learn to monitor their comprehension.
- **Main ideas.** Main ideas are usually expressed in one sentence. Explicitly teach students how to express the main idea of a reading selection, and provide opportunities for them to practice telling or writing main ideas.
- **Summarizing.** Summarizing is an important comprehension skill. If students can summarize information in their own words, they understand what they have

TABLE 4.4   Story-Reading Guide

STORY TITLE	INFORMATION FROM THE STORY
Story Elements	
Setting (time and place)	
Characters (main characters)	
Key events	

read. Teach students how to summarize paragraphs and passages, and provide opportunities for them to practice summarization skills.

- **Prior knowledge.** Help activate prior knowledge by relating what students are learning to previously learned information.
- **Comprehension repairing.** Teach students what to do when they do not comprehend what they are reading (e.g., ask for help, re-read the passage, look up unfamiliar words).
- **Use bypass reading.** If a student understands reading material when the text is read to him or her, use bypass reading. Bypass reading is reading the material to the student. This can be accomplished by the teacher reading the text or reading material, assigning a peer to read to the student, or by providing tapes or audio files of reading selections (Dyck & Pemberton, 2002). This accommodation should be used to allow a student to access content material and should not replace reading instruction if the student needs instruction to improve reading skills.

Suggestions for Culturally or Linguistically Diverse Students

The greatest challenge linguistically diverse students face in school is learning a new language. First, they must understand a new "sound system" or spoken English before they can begin to read in this new language. Even a subject such as mathematics uses many terms foreign to English speakers, let alone English language learners (ELLs). For example, fourth-grade mathematics vocabulary includes terms such as perpendicular, obtuse angle, first quadrant, and rotational symmetry.

Teachers need to know their ELLs' literacy skill levels in their primary language. If ELLs are not competent readers in their primary language then they will be learning a second language while trying to master literacy skills. On the other hand, students who are literate in their native language should be able to transfer their literacy skills to their new language (Jesness, 2004).

Other diverse students who are not ELLs may also have a difficult time learning to read. Background knowledge is a large part of reading. Even if students can decode and understand the meaning of individual words they will not understand the reading passage if they have insufficient background knowledge and experience.

Below we present some suggestions for ELLs with disabilities. The discussion and bulleted suggestions are only a few of the possibilities available to teachers. We strongly recommend teachers access additional resources, such as English as a second language specialists in the schools, to supplement these few suggestions.

Select Printed Materials from Students' Cultural Perspectives.   Students will be more motivated to learn to read when they are excited about the content they will be reading. Comprehension of textual materials is greatly enhanced when students can relate to the content they are reading. Many juvenile books are available that portray, for example, immigrant, migrant, and international families. Work with your school or public librarian to identify appropriate books for the students in your classroom. Many culture-specific lists are available; Table 4.5 provides a list of books about Asian culture.

Provide Opportunities for Students to Connect with Literature, Including Listening to Stories Read Aloud.   Students of all ages enjoy listening to a good story. Often, students' listening comprehension is greater than their reading comprehension. So, when teachers read aloud, students are introduced to literary qualities, including vocabulary that is more sophisticated than their ability to read. This is particularly important for ELLs. Engage them in meaningful discussions about books read, and relate books and stories to the students and their experiences.

TABLE 4.5   Books about Asian Culture

BOOK TITLE AND AUTHOR	TYPE OF BOOK
Almond Cookies and Dragon Well Tea by Cynthia Chin Lee	Chinese-American picture book
Chachaji's Cup by Uma Krishnaswami	Asian Indian picture book
Jin Woo by Eve Bunting	Korean American picture book
Rice is Life by Rita Golden Gelamn	Indonesian informational book
Children of the Dragon: Selected Tales from Vietnam by Sherry Garland	Vietnamese folklore
Confucius: The Golden Rule by Russell Freeman	Chinese biography
Everything you Need to Know about Asian American History and Culture by Himilee Novas and Lan Cao	Pan-Asian informational
Kira-Kira by Cynthia Kadohata	Japanese American fiction

Encourage Students to Explore Alphabet Books. Alphabet books describe the alphabet in unique and interesting ways. These books can help students become more acquainted with letter names and words that begin with various sounds. The best books for this purpose have enjoyable pictures of words that the ELL already knows (Ariza, 2006). Although alphabet books are often thought of as appropriate only for young children, many sophisticated illustrated alphabet books exist that are actually more appropriate for older learners. Students can also be exposed to books that portray a culture with which they are familiar but that use the English language or multilanguages. In Table 4.6, we provide a sample list of books.

Use a Brief Word Association Task to Assess Students' Prior Knowledge. Provide students with a phrase that relates to the topic they will be reading (e.g., "Humans need water."). Ask them to say or write (depending on their skill level) as many words or

---

TABLE 4.6 Sample Alphabet Books Depicting Various Cultures

Africa

- *A is for Africa* by Ifeoma Onyefulo, Puffin, 1997.
- *An African ABC* by Jacqui Taylor, Struik, 2003.
- *Ashanti to Zulu: African Traditions* by Margaret Musgrove & Diane Dillon, Puffin, 1992.

Asian and South Asian

- *A to Zen: A Book of Japanese Culture* by Ruth Wells & Yoshi, Simon & Schuster, 1992.
- *D is for Doufu: An Alphabet Book of Chinese Culture* by Maywan Shen Krach & Hongbin Zhang, Shen's Book, 2000.
- *I is for India* by Prodeepta Das, Frances Lincoln, 2000.

Caribbean and Pacific Islands

- *Hawaiian Alphabet* by Lori Phillips, Bess, 2004.
- *J is for Jamaica* by Benjamin Zephaniah & Prodeepta Das, Frances Lincoln, 2006.

Latino

- *Abecedarios: Mexican Folk Art, ABCs in Spanish and English* by Cynthia Weill, Armando Jimenez, & K. B. Basseches, Cinco Puntos, 2007.
- *F is for Fiesta* by Susan Middleton Elya & G. Brian Karas, Putnam, 2006.
- *Gathering the Sun: An Alphabet in Spanish and English* by Alma Flor Ada & Simon Silva, Rayo, 2001.

Middle Eastern

- *Jewish Alphabet* by Janet Clement & Albert G. Rodriguez, Pelican, 2006.
- *My First Arabic Alphabet* by Siddiqa Juma, Tahrike Tarsile Quran, 2000.
- *P is for Pakistan* by Shazia Razzak & Prodeepta Das, Frances Lincoln, 2007.

phrases that relate to this statement in three minutes. Then write the entire list of student-generated words on the board. Assign students to free write on this topic for five minutes. Tell them not to worry about their grammar, spelling, or punctuation. This will provide you with an assessment of their prior knowledge so you can determine what needs to be pretaught prior to reading about this topic (Farrell, 2006).

During Prereading, Provide Students with the Background Information They Might Need. This is particularly important when students are struggling with decoding skills. Another option is to avoid text material that requires prior knowledge students do not have.

Provide a Brief Outline or Summary of the Story or Chapter Ahead of Time. When students are provided a guide in advance, they are more likely to follow the overall story or reading passage although they may not understand all the words. Other students could be assigned to provide this information to ELLs, if appropriate.

Explicitly Teach Reading Behaviors such as How to Respond to Questions. When teachers explicitly teach reading behaviors, students learn that literacy expectations at school may differ from language experiences in their homes and communities. For example, when discussing stories in class, teachers often ask known-answer questions (literal questions with obvious answers). For some students, answering known-answer questions is unfamiliar language behavior. "In African American communities, the expression of obvious information—stating what 'everyone already knows'—is not considered appropriate or skilled verbal behavior" (Meir, 2003 p. 248). It is therefore important for teachers to explicitly teach students language expectations at school. Teach expectations and explain to students why specific behaviors are important (e.g., answering literal comprehension questions helps the teacher to assess comprehension).

WRITING

Most students with mild to moderate disabilities are expected to participate in writing activities in their classes, to successfully pass district and state writing tests, and to meet the same graduation writing requirements as their nondisabled peers. However, the writing skills of students with disabilities are often far below those of their peers; this is significant considering that most school-aged children are not very competent writers (Englert, Zhao, Dunsmore, Collings, & Wolbers, 2007; Schumaker & Deschler, 2003).

Possible Difficulties with Writing

Many students with mild to moderate disabilities have difficulty with simple mechanical tasks such as spelling, sentence formation, capitalization, punctuation, and handwriting. They also struggle using higher-order cognitive processes when planning, organizing, and revising their written work (Schumaker & Deschler, 2003). They generally take longer to translate ideas into meaning, believe that good writing is limited to correct spelling and legible handwriting, have insufficient vocabulary to communicate their ideas, make transcription and grammar errors, and require more practice to become proficient writers (Prater, 2007).

Most of the strategies reported in the literature to teach students with mild to moderate disabilities focus on self-regulation, motivation, and peer support (De La Paz, 2007). Although cognitive strategy instruction is not used often, it is supported for a wide variety of learners. Cognitive strategies typically include five elements: (1) teachers demonstrate think-alouds, (2) teachers provide explicit instruction and gradually fade instructional scaffolds, (3) students first work collaboratively then independently, (4) teachers transfer regulation of the use of learning strategies to the students, and (5) teachers use mnemonics to help students remember the sequence of steps to execute each strategy and then students execute the learning strategy (De La Paz, 2007). Many of the suggestions below are examples of cognitive learning strategies.

Accommodations and Adaptations that Address Writing Difficulties

Accommodations and adaptations for students with disabilities should align with students' challenges. If students need instruction in writing mechanics, instruction should be adapted for the students. Accommodations can address problems with writing fluency, and incorporating writing strategies in instruction can help students with disabilities acquire writing skills.

Explicitly Teach Handwriting Skills.   Teach students how to sit properly, place paper on the writing surface, use an appropriate pencil grip, and form letters correctly and legibly. When teaching students handwriting, teach one letter at a time so students can master formation, size, spacing, alignment, slant, and production rate. Always model correct letter formation, give students many opportunities for practice in a variety of activities, and provide feedback on their legibility and fluency (Prater, 2007). In addition, make sure that handwriting instruction and expectations for handwritten work are the same in general education and in special education classrooms.

Give Students Pencil Grips and Slant Boards to Use when Writing.   Pencil grips help students to use a proper finger grip on their pencils and can be eliminated once this motor habit is developed. Slant boards help students to connect the visual with the motor task of writing.

Provide wide-ruled paper for students who have problems staying within the lines of college-ruled paper. When students have difficulty with fine motor skills, it is challenging for them to keep their letters within the lines of college-ruled paper. Wide-ruled paper provides more writing space and makes it easier for students to orient their writing within printed lines.

Provide Alternatives to Handwriting.   Some students have hand-eye coordination difficulties that inhibit their ability to write legibly. For such students, teach them to use hardware or software for their written work. Alternatives to pencil and paper include speech recognition software, alternative keyboards, and portable word processors, such as the Neo, which can be used to wirelessly transfer text from student to teacher with a single keystroke (Barbetta & Spears-Bunton, 2007).

Integrate Spelling Instruction with Reading Instruction. When you teach a new vocabulary word you will authentically reinforce its application when students are required to know the word's spelling (Prater, 2007).

Use Multisensory Activities to Teach Spelling Words. Let students see, hear, read out loud, spell out loud, trace, write, proof using a model, and write the word without a model (Prater, 2007). Table 4.7 illustrates how to teach spelling words using a multi-sensory approach.

Give Students Fewer Words to Memorize Until they Reach Mastery. Shorter spelling lists will help students focus on the words they need to master before learning to spell other words.

Teach Students to Use an Inspection Strategy to Find and Correct Spelling Errors Using a Computerized Spellchecker. Teach students how to start the spellchecker function in their word-processing program or with specific software (e.g., Co:Writer). Teach

TABLE 4.7 Multisensory Spelling Instruction

SPELLING INSTRUCTION	PRIMARY SENSES USED
1. "You will learn to spell *nation*."	Auditory
2. "Read and spell this word." The teacher points to the word *nation* written on the board, and the students orally read and spell the word.	Visual, Oral
3. "Trace and spell the word *nation*." Students are given a spelling worksheet and students trace the word and spell it as they trace.	Visual, Tactile, Oral
4. "Write the word *nation* under your traced word." Students write the word nation below their traced word.	Visual, Tactile
5. "Proof and correct your work." Students touch each letter of the traced word as they spell the word. Then, they touch and spell the word they wrote. If they made any errors, they correct them.	Visual, Tactile, Oral
6. "Fold your paper in half and write the word *nation*." Students fold their papers so that they cannot see their traced and written words. Students write nation from memory.	Tactile

students to choose the correctly spelled word from several options. If the correct option is not listed, teach students to sound out the word and try alternative spellings (e.g., *then* or *than*). It is also important to teach students to analyze words they frequently misspell and to teach them specific strategies for preventing recurring errors (e.g., *i* before *e* except after *c*) (Schumaker & Deschler, 2003).

Teach Students How to Use Software to Check Their Grammar.   Most word-processing programs have grammar-checking functions. Also, software packages such as Co:Writer provide word choices that are grammatically correct (Barbetta & Spears-Bunton, 2007).

Teach Students to Use Word Prediction Software.   Some software programs are designed to predict frequently used words based on the context of each sentence and individual students' writing styles. When a student types the beginning of the word, the program automatically provides alternatives to complete the word. The program Co:Writer (mentioned above) has word prediction capabilities (Barbetta & Spears-Bunton, 2007).

Provide Students with Access to Voice Recognition Software.   Voice recognition software converts spoken language to written text. Using this type of software helps students with writing disabilities express themselves without being hindered by limited writing ability. For example, Dragon NaturallySpeaking is a voice recognition program.

Use Prompt Sheets to Teach Students How to Write Basic Statement, Question, Exclamation, and Command/Request Sentences.   Prompt sheets provide structure for writing sentences. Table 4.8 is an example of a prompt sheet to teach basic sentence structures.

Teach a Sentence Writing Strategy to Write Simple, Compound, Complex, and Compound-Complex Sentences.   Teach students to choose a sentence structure, explore words to fit that structure, write the words, and check the sentence for completeness

TABLE 4.8   Prompt Sheet for Basic Sentence Structures

STATEMENT	TYPE OF SENTENCE	EXAMPLE
You like to play soccer.	**Do you** like to play soccer?	Question
	You like to play soccer!	Exclamation
	You will like to play soccer.	Command/Request

TABLE 4.9   Sentence Structure Graphic Organizer

SENTENCE STRUCTURE TABLE	
Simple Sentence	
The subject is a person or thing.	**The predicate includes a verb (action word).**
The horse ⟶	ran.
Bob the baker ⟶	baked.

(Schumaker & Deschler, 2003). Use tables to help students learn the structure of different types of sentences (see Table 4.9).

Provide Feedback Regarding Students' Written Ideas and Separate These Comments from Their Handwriting, Spelling, or Grammar Skills.   Students will feel more confident in their written expression when teachers encourage them to put their thoughts in writing and de-emphasize the lower-order processing difficulties often found in their writing. However, when focusing on the mechanics of writing, you should teach and provide corrective feedback for these skills.

Use Mnemonic Strategies to Help Students Develop Their Persuasive or Expository Writing Skills.   For example, the TREE strategy prompts students to:

- Provide a **T**opic sentence;
- Provide **R**easons for their opinion;
- **E**xamine the reason from the audience's perspective; and
- Provide an **E**nding (Graham & Harris, 1989).

Use Mnemonic Strategies to Help Students in the Prewriting Phase to Generate Ideas from Multiple Perspectives.   Refer to the cognitive strategy instructional model described earlier in this section for a broad perspective on including mnemonics in your instruction. Two cognitive writing strategies, the STOP and DARE strategies, help students to:

- **S**uspend judgment;
- **T**ake a side;
- **O**rganize ideas; and
- **P**lan as they write more,

as well as including these essential elements in their essays:

- **D**evelop a topic sentence;
- **A**dd supporting ideas;
- **R**eject possible arguments for the other side; and
- **E**nd with a conclusion (De La Paz & Graham, 1997). See Table 4.10 for an example of using the DARE strategy to plan a written assignment on health and nutrition.

TABLE 4.10   DARE Strategy Example

WRITING ASSIGNMENT: HEALTH AND NUTRITION	
Develop a topic sentence	Healthy eating habits are important for preventing health problems.
Add supporting ideas	1. Healthy eating habits for most teenagers include eating daily at least 3 oz. whole grains, 2–3 cups of vegetables, 1–2 cups of fruit, 3 cups of dairy, 5–6 oz. of meat and beans, and very few fats. 2. Eating healthy foods helps you prevent cancer, heart disease, stroke, type II diabetes, cataracts, high blood pressure, asthma, bronchitis, and osteoporosis. 3. The food pyramid (www.mypyramid.gov) helps you determine your own recommended eating guidelines.
Reject possible arguments for the other side	1. Some people believe you can eat whatever you want when you are young because you won't get fat and unhealthy until you're older. Research shows us that this is not true because we develop our eating habits when we are young. 2. Some people think that you can be healthy by not eating certain foods like carbohydrates or fruits. Again, most research supports a balanced daily diet instead of a limited one.
End with a conclusion	If we eat according to our own Food Pyramid guidelines, then we are more likely to develop healthy eating habits that can last a lifetime and we will be less likely to have certain health problems.

Teach Students to Use Graphic Organizers in the Prewriting Stage.   Software programs such as Inspiration or Kidspiration can be used to help students make graphic connections between and among their ideas. With this software they can record their words into their projects, including symbols, pictures, video, and sound files, which supports various types of learners (Barbetta & Spears-Bunton, 2007). See Figure 4.4 for an example of a graphic organizer for writing a biographical essay.

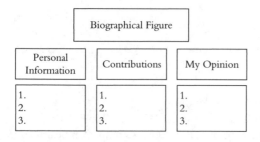

FIGURE 4.4   Biographical Essay Graphic Organizer.

TABLE 4.11   Biographical Essay Outline Example

Biographical Essay
I.   Personal Information
        A. When born:
        B. Where born:
        C. When died:
        D. Where died:
        E.
        F.
II. Significant Contributions
        A.
        B.
        C.
III. My Opinions
        A.
        B.
        C.

Teach Students to Develop and Follow an Outline for Their Writing.   Software programs such as Inspiration and Kidspiration convert graphic organizers to outlines. See Table 4.11 for an example of an outline for writing a biographical essay.

Teach Students to Use Reference Support Materials.   Teach students how to look up facts, definitions, or other information from traditional reference sources such as a dictionary, encyclopedia, and thesaurus. Teach them how to use electronic reference technologies such as Internet-based dictionaries, encyclopedias, or hardware such as the Merriam-Webster Speaking Dictionary and Thesaurus (Barbetta & Spears-Bunton, 2007).

Teach Students to Use a Theme-Writing Strategy.   The theme-writing strategy helps students to compose well-organized and integrated themes or topics for complex writing tasks. Teach students to write what they know about a topic, gather additional information, and organize their information. Then have students write an introductory paragraph, at least three paragraphs with details, and one concluding paragraph. Remind students to attend to transitions between paragraphs and to use their sentence writing strategy, paragraph writing strategy, and error monitoring or inspection strategy (Schumaker & Deschler, 2003).

Ask Critical Questions to Evaluate the Structure of a Written Argument.   For example, ask, "What evidence do you have to support your thesis?" and "Are there other consequences that might happen if we follow your proposal?" (Ferretti, Andrews-Weckerly, & Lewis, 2007).

Teach Students to Use the AutoSummarize Function in Their Word-Processing Program.
AutoSummarize selects main ideas from each paragraph. Students can be taught to com-
pare their intended main idea with the idea(s) selected by the computer (Barbetta &
Spears-Bunton, 2007).

*Teach an Error-Monitoring Strategy to Help Students Find and Correct Their Writ-
ing Errors.*   Teach students to proofread their work by having them write a rough
draft using every other line on the paper, and then to check their work for organizational, spelling, and grammatical errors. Students can be taught strategies for
proofing their work (e.g., Ninja Turtles Counting Pizza Toppings is a mnemonic
strategy for checking for Name, Title, Capitalization, Punctuation, and Transition
words) (Buchan et al., 1996). After students have proofread their work, have them
recopy their work, attending to their notes prior to submitting their work to the
teacher (Schumaker & Deschler, 2003).

Suggestions for Culturally or Linguistically Diverse Students

Students who have disabilities and are culturally or linguistically diverse have many
obstacles to overcome in order to become effective communicators via written
expression. First, although they may have sufficient verbal language for their daily
activities, they may not have requisite skills to communicate their thoughts in writing.
Also, because of their disability, they may learn written expression in a different way or
at a different pace than their nondisabled peers. Finally, they may not receive modeling
and support at home for expressing themselves in writing.

Because of these obstacles, teachers should individualize their instruction to
meet the needs of students with mild to moderate disabilities who are culturally or linguistically diverse.

Be Aware that Writing Conventions May Be Different in a Student's Culture.   What
is considered good writing in one culture may be different from what is considered
good writing in the dominant culture. For example, in some cultures, writers may not
be as direct in expressing ideas and discussing topics. English-speaking writers typically
use a standard structure for composing essays and compositions (i.e., topic sentences,
supporting details, concluding statements, and transition sentences). Writers from
other cultures may not follow these conventions, and may instead indirectly express
their thoughts.

Create Mixed-Ability Writing Groups.   Give writing assignments to groups who can
discuss their ideas and work collaboratively on the writing assignment. Provide verbal
and written feedback to each group.

Allow Students to Discuss Writing Assignments in Their Primary Language.   Students
can clarify and explain concepts to one another in their primary language prior to
producing their written work.

Prompt Students to Create an Outline in Their Primary Language. Writing a draft in their primary language helps students to organize their thoughts before thinking and writing their papers in English.

Choose Writing Assignments that Are Student-Oriented. Writing assignments that are of interest to culturally and linguistically diverse (CLD) students are more likely to elicit thoughtful responses than are assignments that they deem unrelated to their home, family, and community.

Choose Spelling Words that Are Relevant to the Students. Rather than using a list of isolated spelling words, select words that are in the students' vocabulary and that are relevant to their life experiences.

MATH

This section will give you suggestions for making appropriate accommodations and adaptations so students can access math instruction effectively. Students with mild to moderate disabilities often have deficits in numerical and arithmetical concepts and processes. Students with mathematics learning disabilities have lower-than-expected math achievement scores over several successive years and often have memory or cognitive deficits. However, many students with mathematics learning disabilities also have reading disabilities and attention deficit/hyperactivity disorder (Geary, 2004).

Possible Difficulties Accessing Mathematics Instruction

Students with impairments in learning math have cognitive performance and patterns that differ from those without these disabilities. For example, they have difficulty retrieving basic arithmetic facts from long-term memory and ignoring extraneous information in word problems. Additionally, students with disabilities frequently struggle to understand problems; they make procedural errors and rely on procedure-based problem solving rather than memory-based problem solving (Geary, 2004; van Garderen & Montague, 2003; Xin, Jitendra, & Deatline-Buchman, 2005). These deficits often result in students using problem-solving procedures that are more typically used by young children (e.g., finger counting).

In addition to having deficits associated with learning problems, some students who struggle to learn mathematic concepts have poorly developed number sense. Number sense refers to the ability to understand numeric relationships. Children with well-developed number sense can quickly estimate and judge magnitude, recognize unreasonable results, mentally compute problems, and understand different representations of numbers (Gersten, Jordan, & Flojo, 2005). Children with poorly developed number sense struggle in all these areas and need instruction to help them acquire skills such as counting and quantity discrimination, which are necessary for understanding math.

Accommodations and Adaptations that Address Difficulty Accessing Mathematics Instruction

Accommodations and adaptations for students who struggle to learn mathematics should focus on attending to these underlying cognitive processes and patterns. Regardless of whether teachers' instructional approaches focus on conceptual understanding or on learning procedures and facts, they must consider the unique learning processes of students with mild to moderate disabilities in order to teach them effectively. Some of the suggestions provided below are found elsewhere in this book; however, examples are provided that relate specifically to the acquisition and retention of mathematic knowledge and skills.

Review Previously Taught Information.   Students who have difficulty with long-term memory retrieval will benefit from frequent reviews of previously learned information. These students need opportunities to demonstrate their prior knowledge rather than merely listening to the teacher provide a verbal review.

Preteach Mathematical Vocabulary.   Since many students with mild to moderate disabilities have difficulty with language-based learning, they may need extra vocabulary instruction. For example, words such as *adjacent, hypotenuse,* and *Pythagorean* may not only be difficult for students to understand but also to read and pronounce (Prater, 2007). Preteaching these words will allow students to focus on the mathematical concepts to be learned rather than on the vocabulary associated with the concepts.

Explicitly Teach Students Skills that Develop Number Sense.   Counting skills are fundamental to developing number sense. Explicitly teach students counting skills such as one-to-one correspondence, counting on (e.g., starting at five and counting three more), counting backwards, and skip counting (Gersten et al., 2005). Use the concrete-representation-abstract sequence (discussed in more detail below) to help students understand counting.

Use the Concrete-Representation-Abstract (CRA) Sequence to Teach Math Concepts and to Help Students Develop a Conceptual Understanding of Mathematic Relationships.
With the CRA sequence, begin teaching concepts and skills using manipulatives (blocks or other objects). Once students master skills or understand concepts using manipulatives, move on to visual representations of the concepts (pictures and tallies). Then, use abstract symbols such as numbers to represent concepts. The following guidelines can help you determine how many lessons you might need to devote to each levels of the CRA sequence.

- Teach three lessons at the concrete level (using manipulatives). At this level, students should achieve at least eighty percent accuracy during independent practice for each lesson.
- Teach three representational lessons (pictures and tallies). Each lesson should consist of approximately twenty problems, and students should achieve eighty

percent accuracy before moving to the abstract level of instruction (Miller & Hudson, 2007).

When using manipulatives and pictures, vary the manipulatives and pictures used (Miller & Hudson, 2007). For example, when teaching addition, you may initially use blocks to teach students that addition is combining groups of objects and counting the combined total. In subsequent lessons at the concrete level, use different objects such as counting bears to teach the concept. By varying objects, students learn that addition is not associated with only blocks. Similarly, when using pictures, vary how concepts are represented using pictures (e.g., blocks and then tally marks). Be sure to use age-appropriate manipulatives—counting bears are appropriate for elementary students but not for secondary students. Also, consider students' fine motor skills using the CRA teaching sequence. Students who have difficulty with fine motor skills may need larger objects or more white space on papers to draw representations of numbers.

Use Appropriate Structures for Teaching Concepts. Concepts can be taught using the following structures: (a) compare/contrast for presenting similarities and differences that illustrate concepts, (b) example/nonexample for teaching students to discriminate between concepts, and (c) step-by-step for teaching sequential steps associated with concepts (Miller & Hudson, 2007). Select the structure that is appropriate for the concept you are teaching. For example, when teaching geometric shapes, the example/nonexample structure would be appropriate to help students learn how to discriminate among different shapes. Use manipulatives to teach students the concept *circle* at the concrete level. When teaching the concept, show students examples of circles and nonexamples (e.g., triangles and squares). At the representation level, have students color examples of circles and cross out nonexamples (see Figure 4.5).

Use Explicit Instruction to Teach Skills Necessary for Conceptual Understanding. Explicit instruction methods are effective strategies for teaching mathematics to students with mild to moderate disabilities. When implementing explicit instruction, present new material in small segments. For example, teach one geometric shape per lesson. Model strategies to solve problems or to apply knowledge, and then provide the practice and feedback necessary to develop accuracy and fluency (Miller & Hudson, 2007). See Appendix A for an example of how to teach the concept of *square* using an explicit instructional approach.

Use Massed Practice During the Acquisition Stage of Learning. Providing ample opportunities for students to practice correct answers will facilitate their shift from using procedural-based strategies to memory-based strategies. However, you must

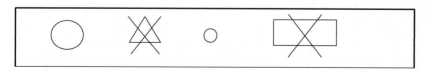

FIGURE 4.5 Example/Nonexample Structure.

ensure that the students are practicing correct answers rather than incorrect answers (e.g., practice $2 + 2 = 4$ rather than $2 + 2 = 5$). You can implement one-minute timings in instruction to provide opportunities for massed practice (Miller & Hudson, 2007). To implement one-minute timings, give students math-fact sheets (called probes) that have more math-fact problems on them than the students can solve in one minute. Probes generally focus on mastering a few math facts at one time (e.g., a probe would have problems from the fact family 2, 4, and 6; $2 + 4 = 6$, $4 + 2 = 6$, $6 - 4 = 2$, $6 - 2 = 4$). Give the students one minute to solve as many problems on the probe as possible. Score the probe, and direct the students to plot the number of correct and incorrect digits on a graph. The graph allows students to see their progress and can motivate them to improve their performance.

Implement Incremental Rehearsal. Incremental rehearsal is a drill and practice routine that combines known facts or information with new information to be learned (Burns, 2005). For example, when learning math facts, students are shown math equations written on 3×5 cards. An unknown fact is introduced as the student reviews and practices other known facts. In the practice sequence, the first fact shown to the student is an unknown fact (e.g., $3 \times 4 = ?$). The student reads the equation and then states the answer. Then, the student rehearses the unknown fact plus other known facts using the sequence illustrated in Table 4.12. After the student completes the entire sequence, the previously unknown fact becomes a known fact, and a new unknown fact can be introduced during a subsequent practice session.

Implement Procedures that Ensure Errorless Learning. Whether you use the incremental rehearsal routine or other procedures to help students learn math facts, ensure errorless learning. Use the Constant Time Delay procedure to prevent student from learning errors (Miller & Hudson, 2007). The procedure involves the following steps:

TABLE 4.12   Incremental Rehearsal Sequence

INCREMENTAL REHEARSAL SEQUENCE

---

1. *Unknown fact* $3 \times 4 =$
   Known fact $2 \times 2 =$

2. *Unknown fact* $3 \times 4 =$
   Known fact $2 \times 2 =$
   Known fact $2 \times 1 =$

3. *Unknown fact* $3 \times 4 =$
   Known fact $2 \times 2 =$
   Known fact $2 \times 1 =$
   Known fact $2 \times 3 =$

4. *Unknown fact* $3 \times 4 =$
   Known fact $2 \times 2 =$
   Known fact $2 \times 1 =$
   Known fact $2 \times 3 =$
   Known fact $2 \times 4 =$

★ Continue the above sequence until the student is shown ten known facts with the one unknown fact.

Source: Adapted from "Using Incremental Rehearsal to Increase Fluency of Single-digit Multiplication Facts with Children Identified as Learning Disabled in Mathematics Computation" by M. K, Burns, *Education and Treatment of Children, 28* (3), 2005, p. 242. Reprinted with permission.

(a) show a student a flash card with a math fact such as $4 + 3 = 7$, (b) give the student three to five seconds to respond, (c) show the next fact ($4 + 4 = 8$) if the student responds correctly, (d) provide the correct response if the student does not answer correctly and then have the student repeat the model ($4 + 3 = 7$).

Provide Fact Sheets when Students Understand Concepts but Are Not Fluent with Math Facts.   Sometimes, it takes students longer to learn math facts than it takes them to understand concepts. If students understand concepts but have not mastered math facts (multiplication facts), provide fact charts for students to use when solving problems. To prevent dependency on the chart for facts already memorized, black out facts as students master facts (Fahsl, 2007).

Teach Students Self-Monitoring Strategies and Self-Talk Strategies for Completing Math Problems.   For example, students can touch and say the name of the operation (e.g., "divided by"), or verbally state the steps while completing the process. Table 4.13 is an example of self-talk steps for solving story problems.

Provide Graph Paper to Help Students Align Columns for Math Problems.   Using this type of a prompt helps those with visual spatial deficits so they can focus on the math concept rather than the spatial orientation of math problems (Fahsl, 2007). If graph paper is not available, students can use wide-ruled paper turned sideways to provide lines for column alignment. Teach students how to organize problems when they use graph paper. For example, teach them to skip a space between the problem number and the problem.

Create Prompt Sheets for Completing Algorithms.   Prompt sheets can be in written format or organized graphically (see Figure 4.6). When creating prompt sheets, use simple, concise language (Miller & Hudson, 2007). Be aware of students with reading deficits who may get stuck on figuring out the written prompts rather than figuring out the mathematical problem. For them, a picture prompt may be more appropriate.

TABLE 4.13   Self-talk Example for Solving Story Problems

SELF-TALK STEPS FOR SOLVING STORY PROBLEMS

---

1. First I read the story problem.
2. Then I underline words that indicate the mathematic operation.
3. After I underline the words, I write the equation.
4. I read the equation and solve the problem.

Roxie <u>had 7 books.</u> She bought <u>4 new books</u> at a bookstore. How many books did she have <u>in all</u>? $7 + 4 = 11$

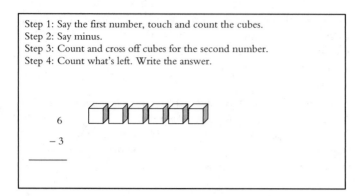

Step 1: Say the first number, touch and count the cubes.
Step 2: Say minus.
Step 3: Count and cross off cubes for the second number.
Step 4: Count what's left. Write the answer.

6
− 3
_____

FIGURE 4.6   Prompt Sheet for Subtraction.

Use a Variety of Presentation Modes, such as Songs to Teach Math Facts.   Many commercial products are available that create songs and movement-based activities to learn math facts. In addition, you can have your students create their own music.

Provide Graphic Organizers, Outlines, and Flow Charts to Introduce and Organize New Information.   Using graphic organizers helps students to visualize concepts, processes, and mathematical rules (see Table 4.14). Focus on relationships when using graphic organizers rather than simply on pictorial representations, as relationship-based representations facilitate more efficient learning (van Garderen & Montague, 2003).

Use Schema–Based Instruction to Facilitate Conceptual Understanding.   Schema-based instruction (SBI) differs from the typical textbook-based general-strategy instruction (GSI). A four-step GSI procedure for problem-solving generally includes (1) read to understand, (2) develop a plan by drawing a picture to represent the problem, (3) solve the problem, and (4) check work. SBI differs because it emphasizes understanding the problem type, structure, and relationships among variables. The relationships are often formed in a visual mental image (van Garderen & Montague, 2003). SBI differs from GSI in steps 2 and 3: (2) "identify the problem type, and use a schema diagram to represent the problem," and (3) "transform the diagram to a math sentence, and solve the

TABLE 4.14   Example of Pictorial and Relationship-Based Representations

PICTORIAL REPRESENTATION	RELATIONSHIP-BASED REPRESENTATION
Drawing of an object or person, such as a man planting two apple trees.	Drawing or a diagram that shows relationships between objects or persons, such as a man planting two apple trees that produce 100 apples each, which are then used to make 20 jars of applesauce.

Problem: If Somsak uses 2 small chili peppers in every bowl of Thai noodles, how many chili peppers does he need to make 4 bowls of noodles? (★ = 1 chili pepper; ^ = 1 bowl of noodles).

★★   ★★   ★★   ★★   Chili peppers

^   ^   ^   ^   Bowls of noodles

Answer: Somsak needs 8 small chili peppers to make 4 bowls of noodles.

FIGURE 4.7   Visual Representation of a Story Problem.

problem" (Xin et al., 2005, p. 184). Using schematic visual representations may facilitate abstract understanding and generalization of skills. Figure 4.7 is an example of a schematic representation of a multiplicative comparison problem.

Teach Students Strategies to Reduce Student Errors.   As you teach students new algorithms, teach them strategies to reduce errors. For example, when teaching students how to calculate the areas of different geometric shapes, teach them to write the formula before they begin to solve the problem. So, before calculating the area of a triangle, students would write $\frac{1}{2}(b \times h)$. They would then fill in the numbers and solve for the area.

Teach Students Strategies that Help them Learn and Remember Procedures for Solving Problems.   When developing procedural strategies, use the following guidelines: (a) include sequence steps for solving the problem, (b) make sure the steps used can be generalized to other problem types, (c) provide an action prompt (add or write) in each step, (d) state each step using as few words as possible, and (e) use a mnemonic device to help students remember the strategy (Miller & Hudson, 2007). Figure 4.8 shows an example of the SAW procedure for solving two-digit plus two-digit problems without regrouping (Miller & Hudson, 2007, p. 52).

Set up to solve.
    Read the problem.
    Identify the sign.
Attack the problem.
    Add the ones column.
    Write the answer in the ones column.
    Add the tens column.
    Write the answer in the tens column.
Wrap it up.
    Check the addition.

FIGURE 4.8   The SAW Procedural Strategy.

Illustrate How Math Concepts Relate to the Students' Lives. Incorporating authentic experiences, such as a classroom store, will help students understand the function of mathematics in everyday life.

Provide Assistive Technology. Although most students with mild to moderate disabilities will obtain basic skills in mathematical calculation, some may still need to use calculators to facilitate efficient responses. When lessons focus on skills wherein calculation is necessary but is not the objective, providing calculators can help these students focus on more complex concepts. Also, graphing calculators and computer spreadsheets can help students visualize mathematical procedures and concepts (Jarrett, 1999).

Suggestions for Culturally or Linguistically Diverse Students

Culturally or linguistically diverse students experience difficulty in learning mathematics due to language, culture, learning modality, cultural dissonance between school and home, and excessively abstract instruction (Reyhner & Davison, 1992). Teachers must attend to these individual differences as they plan, deliver, and assess instruction. The following suggestions are specific to students with mild to moderate disabilities who are culturally or linguistically diverse.

Be Aware that Students May Have Learned a Different Way to Do Math Operations in Their Country of Origin. In addition, they may have been taught math skills in a different order. These students may not need to learn a new way of completing mathematical operations as long as the results are the same.

Point Out to Students that Some Words in Their First Language Are Similar to the English Words for Math Concepts. For example, in Spanish the word multiply is *multiplicar.* Other similar English and Spanish words are *fracciones* (fractions), *nimerador* (numerator), and *divider* (divide). Take advantage of these similarities when using these mathematical terms.

Use Culturally Relevant Examples in the Mathematics Curriculum. For instance, some CLD students may perceive adding fourteen to thirty seven as meaningless. However, the problem may become more relevant if it is restructured as the addition of fourteen horses to thirty seven horses in a community where horses are an integral part of daily life (Reyhner & Davison, 1992).

Have CLD Students Create Their Own Word Problems. Often, students do not relate to the situations provided in teacher-generated or textbook word problems. This is particularly true for CLD students. Therefore, allow students to create their own problems. For example, cooperative-learning groups could be assigned to write story problems from which you, as the teacher, will use on the assignment or test. Using personal examples helps activate the students' prior knowledge and experiences, and motivates them to understand the processes involved in their problems (Prater, 2007; Reyhner & Davison, 1992).

SCIENCE

Some students may lack confidence in their ability to succeed in science; however, it should be noted that students are not classified as having a disability because of their poor performance in learning or applying science concepts or skills. Instead, students with mild to moderate disabilities are likely to lack foundational skills necessary for succeeding in the science curriculum (e.g., reading, understanding abstract concepts, remembering information). For example, if a science teacher requires her students to obtain most information through reading and listening to lectures, then her students with reading disabilities, attention difficulties, and problems with abstract concept formation may be hindered from succeeding in learning scientific concepts, principles, and procedures. In this section we provide suggestions for making appropriate accommodations and adaptations so students can access science instruction effectively.

Possible Difficulties Accessing Science Instruction

Four common curricular approaches to teaching science include spiral, intensified, integrated, and theme-based (Cawley, Foley, & Miller, 2003). Each will be discussed briefly, with considerations for using these approaches to teach students with mild to moderate disabilities.

The spiral curriculum is the most common model of science instruction in elementary schools. This type of curriculum is generally textbook-driven, with a standard scope and sequence of science lessons and experiences, and roughly the same amount of time is allotted for each topic (Cawley et al., 2003). In addition, this traditional method usually requires students to listen to lectures, discuss new concepts and vocabulary, answer chapter questions, and take end-of-chapter or unit tests (Prater, 2007). This model is difficult for elementary and secondary students with disabilities because of the heavy reliance on reading, writing, memory, and abstract concept development.

The intensified curriculum tends to use an activity-based approach, generally exploring fewer concepts in more depth rather than covering many topics within the school year (Cawley et al., 2003). It is often based on student inquiry, in which students learn concepts through concrete, hands-on experiences (Prater, 2007). Inquiry-based approaches involve investigating real-life activities or problems, exploring new ideas and formulating questions, finding answers to posed questions, and drawing conclusions that can be applied to different situations (Prater, 2007). Students with disabilities have reported that they enjoy hands-on learning activities more than text-based learning, and that they learn more through active exploration than from textbook instruction (Mastropieri, Scruggs, & Magnusen, 1999). However, students with lower cognitive abilities may experience difficulty learning from inquiry learning. With inquiry methods, students must use problem solving and higher-order thinking skills when they analyze problems and draw conclusions. While this approach minimizes language and literacy requirements, some students with disabilities may need instructional accommodations and adaptations to help them learn how to solve problems and to think critically. They may also need assistance to stay on task, use manipulative materials appropriately, follow classroom rules, and to understand the main point of the activities (Mastropieri et al., 1999).

The integrated curricular approach combines science with another topic, usually mathematics. Using these procedures, the scope and sequence of topics are limited; therefore, teachers often use this to supplement spiral curricular approaches (Cawley et al., 2003). The integrated approach may be beneficial to students with mild to moderate disabilities because it promotes generalization of concepts across topics. However, if these methods are used as a primary method rather than as a supplementary method, then students may lack necessary conceptual knowledge for further advancement in science.

Finally, the theme-based curricular approach uses specific themes to organize science instruction. For example, themes such as change, systems, motion, and energy may cross the topics of life, physical, and earth sciences. Using a theme-based approach is likely to help students with disabilities to understand the theme and connect it to different parts of the science program (Cawley et al., 2003). Since thematic instruction focuses on a few main ideas, it may not appear to be overwhelming for students with memory or processing problems (Steele, 2004).

Accommodations and Adaptations that Address Problems Accessing Science Instruction

Regardless of the curricular approach taken, specific accommodations and adaptations may still be necessary to sufficiently meet the needs of students with mild to moderate disabilities. It is insufficient to simply introduce facts or to expose students to hands-on activities without teaching the conceptual knowledge necessary for comprehension of science processes, principles, and concepts (McCleery & Tindal, 1999). The suggestions listed below are related directly to accessing the science curriculum.

Structure the Class to Promote Positive Student Behaviors.   Although rules are important for any type of instruction, they are critical when teaching science. Students need to understand behavior expectations when engaged in student-led learning activities. Teach them the rules for handling equipment, how to follow safety precautions, how to work appropriately with other students, and then check their understanding of the expectations before beginning the activities.

Teach New Vocabulary Prior to Beginning a New Lesson.   All fields of study have subject-specific vocabulary. In science courses, the number of new vocabulary words students have to learn can be quite large—as many as 300 new words a year in sixth grade to over 3,000 new terms per year in tenth grade (Woodward & Noell, 1991). Prior to teaching daily lessons, teach students the vocabulary they will be exposed to

TABLE 4.15   Teaching Science Vocabulary Using Keywords

VOCABULARY WORD	KEYWORD	DEFINITION	ILLUSTRATION
airborne	air	Carried by air	Things in the air, carried by air
extraterrestrial	ET	From outside earth	ET outside earth
specimens	inspect	Part of a sample to study	A sample to study, being inspected
ionosphere	atmosphere	A layer of the earth's atmosphere	Atmosphere, with ionosphere

Source: From "Keywords Make the Difference! Mnemonic Instruction in Inclusive Classrooms" by H. Z. Uberti, T. E. Scruggs, and M. A. Mastropieri, *TEACHING Exceptional Children, 35,* 2003, 56–61. Copyright 2003 by the Council for Exceptional Children. Reprinted with permission.

during the lesson. Also, teach them strategies for remembering definitions. Table 4.15 illustrates how science vocabulary can be taught using keywords.

Use Explicit Instruction to Teach Skills Necessary for Scientific Inquiry.   The scientific method involves (a) making observations and identifying problems, (b) gathering data, (c) predicting outcomes, (d) designing and conducting experiments, and (e) drawing conclusions and making generalizations. Explicitly teach students the skills they need to work through each step of the scientific method. Analyze each task into short, concise steps, and then model the steps and provide feedback and correction as students practice the process. Table 4.16 provides a task analysis of steps of the scientific method.

Use Structured Questioning Techniques to Help Students Construct Meaning from Inquiry-Based Activities.   Since many students with disabilities experience difficulty with forming abstract concepts and retrieving relevant information from their prior knowledge, you may need to provide additional levels of structure to your inquiry-based teaching (McCleery & Tindal, 1999). Provide specific rather than general questions for students to examine, along with teacher or student prompting or coaching to guide their meaning. For example, after explicitly teaching phases and states of matter, you might engage the students in a hands-on activity in which they examine the properties of household items such as ketchup, perfume, water, and soda. You could then extend the activity by asking questions such as: "Do the various forms of matter we have studied exist only in those forms?" (Cawley et al., 2003. p. 168), and have students conduct an activity to illustrate this principle (e.g., water turning to ice).

Provide Graphic Organizers, Outlines, and Flow Charts to Introduce and Organize New Information.   Using graphic organizers helps students to visualize concepts, processes, and scientific rules. Graphic organizers help students attend to relevant information from textbooks or other sources of complex information. Graphic organizers

TABLE 4.16   Task Analysis for the Scientific Method

SCIENTIFIC METHOD	TASK ANALYSIS
Problem	■ Make an observation. ■ Write a question about your observation.
Hypothesis	■ Write down what you already know about the problem or question. ■ Using what you know, make a guess about what you think will happen in your experiment. ■ Write the hypothesis as a complete sentence.
Method	■ List materials used. ■ Write down each step of your experiment as you complete your experiment.
Results	■ Write down the results (the actual numbers). ■ Plot the results on a graph. ■ Write a three to five sentence summary of the results.
Conclusions	■ Based on your results, decide if your hypothesis was correct. ■ Write a paragraph about how the results supported your hypothesis. ■ If the results did not support your hypothesis, write a paragraph about why you think your hypothesis was not correct.

can be partially completed or include prompts to help students develop skills in creating their own outlines or organizers (Watson & Johnston, 2007). For example, the scientific method can be taught using a graphic organizer that has prompts to stimulate thinking (McCleery & Tindal, 1999). Figure 4.9 is an example of a graphic organizer with prompts.

Explicitly Teach Relationships Between Concepts and Principles.   If students understand how concepts and principles are related, it is easier for them to generalize learning across subjects and topics. Concepts share defining attributes, and when students identify attributes of concepts, they can apply their knowledge to different situations. For example, gases are substances that disperse evenly in containers. Students must identify attributes of gases (e.g., dispersion, volume, substance) in order to discriminate between substances that are gases and substances that are not. Principles reflect conceptual relationships and are stated in *if-then* format such as *if a gas is heated, then it expands* (McCleery & Tindal, 1999). This principle can be applied to geophysics, astronomical phenomena, and thermal dynamics associated with weather patterns. By teaching the concept in conjunction with the principle, critical information is highlighted and reading demands may be reduced.

Use a Variety of Methods to Teach New Concepts.   Use lecture time to teach concepts and to clarify misconceptions, and then use a variety of other teaching methods to

Date _____

Name _____   Experiment # _____

Observation and problem:

Write down what you observed about the air around a light bulb. Write a question about air around light bulbs.

Observation

_____

_____

Problem

_____

_____

Hypothesis

Write your guess about what will happen when you conduct your experiment.

_____

_____

Materials and Procedures

List the materials you will use for the experiment and describe the procedures for conducting your experiment. Write each step as you perform each step.

Materials

_____

_____

Procedures
   1.
   2.
   3.
   4.

Results

Write the results of the experiment. Record numbers and measurements and/or describe what happened as a result of the experiment.

_____

FIGURE 4.9   Graphic Organizer with Prompts.

make learning meaningful. Incorporate cooperative learning activities, discussions, observations, hands-on activities, demonstrations, videos, and reflection (Steele, 2007).

Use Computer-Assisted Instruction to Supplement Daily Lessons.   Many software packages are available commercially or online. For example, at the Virtual Cell web site, students can manipulate animal cells to explore the nature of different organelles or areas of the cell (www.ibiblio.org/virtualcell/index.htm). Often, these web sites include worksheets for students to use while investigating scientific concepts (Watson & Johnston, 2007).

Use Digital Libraries to Access Information.   Many digital libraries are available, and with text-to-speech software, students with disabilities can access the written word more easily. Examples of these libraries include BiosciEdNet (www.biosciednet.org), National Science Digital Library (http://nsdl.org), and Digital Library for Earth System Education (www.dlese.org) (Curry, Cohen, & Lightbody, 2006).

Use Accessible Laboratory and Field Equipment.   Computer-controlled laboratory equipment facilitates accessible learning for all students, as the hardware interacts with software to control timing of measurements, and record or display data throughout the experiment. For example, meters with auditory readouts, talking thermometers, probes, digital cameras, digital voice recorders, sensors, and other devices can be used to help students engage in the scientific learning environment (Curry, 2006).

Facilitate Inquiry-Based Learning by Using WebQuests.   WebQuests are online research methods that can be individualized to stimulate students to ask relevant questions and find answers via the Web (see http://webquest.sdsu.edu). For example, to complete a WebQuest related to the National Science Education Content Standard D for Grades 9–12: "All students should develop an understanding of energy in the Earth system," you can have students hypothesize what they expect to happen during their investigation of a local park, have them simulate a field investigation, and then ask them to access the NASA earth science web site (http://science, hq.nasa.gov/education/index.html) to obtain information about this content standard (Curry et al., 2006).

Teach Mnemonic Strategies.   Teach students how to use mnemonic strategies to help them remember science information. For example, the acronym ROY G BIV represents the first letter of the colors in the spectrum (red, orange, yellow, green, blue, indigo, violet) (Jarrett, 1999).

Provide Reading Support for Text-Based Learning.   If you rely on textbooks to deliver information to students, be sure to ensure that those with reading difficulties can access the information in a different format or with the type of assistance each student needs. See Part II–Accessing Printed Information for specific ideas to accommodate reading difficulties.

Vary How Learning is Assessed.   Your assessment should directly align with the objective(s) for each lesson or unit. If students have reading or writing difficulties, their performance on a written test may not accurately reflect what they learned. Therefore, design your tests to measure their acquisition and retention of scientific knowledge, not their reading or writing skills. Options include projects, oral and written reports, problem-solving activities, portfolios, and concept maps (Steele, 2004).

Suggestions for Culturally or Linguistically Diverse Students

Culturally or linguistically diverse students who have mild or moderate disabilities encounter obstacles accessing the science curriculum. However, as noted by the American Association for the Advancement of Science, "All students with disabilities have potential in science" (Jarrett, 1999, p. 14), and teachers must convey their confidence in the abilities of all their students. First and foremost, teachers must develop a trusting, respectful relationship with students, understanding their backgrounds and life circumstances, in order to plan and deliver meaningful learning activities. Teachers must be able to convey that they care about their students, want them to succeed, know that their English proficiency is not indicative of intelligence, and see each student as a potential contributor to scientific knowledge (Dobb, 2004).

In addition to the suggestions made for students with mild to moderate disabilities, the following suggestions are specific to those who are CLD.

Teach Vocabulary Necessary for Understanding New Concepts.   Realize that CLD students may have social or "playground" language, but their academic language, particularly in science, may hinder them from understanding the abstract language of textbooks. Therefore, they may need additional instruction in vocabulary words or terms that are rarely encountered.

Use Teacher Manuals or Guides that Accompany Science Textbooks.   These manuals often include suggestions for teaching science to CLD students. Note that the suggestions provided often require full integration of CLD strategies into the science curriculum and should not be considered additive or supplementary (Dobb, 2004).

Integrate Inquiry-Based Activities in Instruction.   Students from diverse backgrounds can become bored easily, particularly if they do not have the academic language and/or experiential background needed for science lessons. They may learn better by inquiry-based activities that do not have a high reliance on linguistic competencies (Reyhner & Davison, 1992).

Use Science Activities that Relate to Students' Out-of-School Lives.   Recognize that scientific worldviews vary among various cultures. Include materials and activities that emphasize concepts or processes from diverse cultures. For example, a lesson can include information about Navajo farming, raising livestock, and traditional use of native plants (Reyhner & Davison, 1992).

SOCIAL STUDIES

The field of social studies includes the integration of many areas: anthropology, archaeology, economics, geography, history, law, philosophy, political science, psychology, religion, and sociology (Prater, 2007). The primary purpose of providing instruction in social studies is to help students become educated citizens who will participate actively in a democratic society (National Council for the Social Studies, 1994). However, curricular approaches differ, with some emphasizing our common national heritage and others emphasizing multiple diverse perspectives of those who inhabit our country (De La Paz & MacArthur, 2003).

Possible Difficulties Accessing Social Studies Instruction

Regardless of the approach to teaching social studies, students with mild to moderate disabilities may need help in accessing the curriculum not because they have a disability in this area, but because their disability in reading, writing, remembering, or other cognitive processes interfere with the acquisition, retention, and generalization of social studies concepts. These difficulties are exacerbated when instruction is heavily reliant on textbook learning, covers too much content, is presented in lecture format, and requires reading levels beyond the ability of these students (Prater, 2007).

Accommodations and Adaptations that Address Problems Accessing Social Studies Instruction

Therefore, accommodations and adaptations in social studies instruction should be targeted toward each student's unique learning characteristics. Some of the suggestions that follow may be found elsewhere in this book; however, specific examples are provided as they relate to teaching social studies to students with mild to moderate disabilities.

Use Cooperative Learning Groups.   Provide students with opportunities to discuss concepts with other students by structuring mixed-ability groups. Be sure to monitor these classroom conversations to immediately clarify misunderstandings or to elaborate on information that is incomplete (Ferretti, MacArthur, & Okolo, 2001).

Review Previously Taught Information.   Students who have difficulty with long-term memory retrieval will benefit from frequent reviews of previously learned information. Ask true/false questions, factual questions, and questions about sequences of historical events to assure all the students have the requisite knowledge to learn the new lesson (Hudson, 1996, 1997).

Relate New Concepts to Relevant Experiences.   Since students may have difficulty relating to anything outside their present experience, it is important to relate the events and people of another time to students' present lives. For example, when discussing the westward migration and religious persecution, teachers can compare and contrast the students' current experiences of religious bias and persecution with those of the Mormon pioneers (Ferretti et al., 2001).

Use Concept Anchoring Routines.   Concept anchoring routines are used to connect new conceptual information with previously learned concepts (Lenz & Schumaker, 1999). An example of a concept anchoring routine to teach the concept of *commensalism* is illustrated in Table 1.3.

Provide Note-Taking Guides for Lectures.   This simple procedure has the potential to increase the understanding and performance of all students because they are able to make sense of the concepts discussed in a lecture. Pause for two to three minutes a few times during the lecture to allow students to ask questions or verbally summarize main ideas in mixed-ability groups of two to three students (Lecture Pause Procedure) (Hudson, 1997). See Figure 4.10 for an example of a note-taking guide. These guides can also be used to record information learned from written texts.

Provide Authentic Problems that Students Confront in Their Life and Work.   When authentic problems are used, there are generally no accepted standards against which

---

New Orleans: A City in Peril?

1. **Sinking City**
   a. *New Orleans is one of the lowest spots in the U.S.*
   b. *17 feet below sea level in places.*
   c. *Sinking up to 1 inch per year.*
   d. *500,000 people living at or below sea level.*

2. **Rising Seas**
   a. *Sea levels may rise several feet over the next century due to global warming.*

3. **Stronger Hurricanes**
   a. *Warm seas increase the number of hurricanes.*
   b. *7–10 hurricanes are predicted for the Atlantic Basin this year.*
   c. *Frequency of monster storms has doubled since 1970.*

4. **Dwindling Wetlands**
   a. *Hurricanes Katrina and Rita took out 217 square miles of wetlands.*

5. **Flawed Levees**
   a. *It may take until 2010 to strengthen the levees to withstand a Category 3 hurricane.*
   b. *Levee effect—dams and levees increase flood losses when they fail because of development in the floodplain.*
   c. *Some floodwalls have not been repaired, floodgates don't clear debris that might keep them from closing.*

FIGURE 4.10   A Completed Note-Taking Guide for Social Studies.

Source: National Geographic, August, 2007.

the solutions are evaluated. Therefore, you should teach students to gather and evaluate available evidence to support their conclusions. For example, to teach students about the Westward migration, present them with a question such as: "Should the miners have gone west?" Then, guide them to find accurate accounts, evaluate bias in these accounts, corroborate sources, and qualify their conclusions (Ferretti et al., 2001).

Use Keyword Strategies to Teach Factual Information. Use a keyword-keyword strategy to teach information such as states and capitols. For example, to teach Topeka as the capital of Kansas, the keyword for Topeka (top) can be associated with the keyword for Kansas (can). The students then visualize a top spinning on a can (Mastropieri, Scruggs, & Whedon, 1997).

Use Pegword Strategies to Teach Factual Information. Associate keywords with pegwords (i.e., rhyming memory device for numbers, such as one = bun, two = shoe). For example, to teach that crocoite has a hardness level of two, associate the keyword for crocoite (crocodile) interacting with a shoe (pegword for two) (Mastropieri et al., 1997).

Use Extended Pegword Strategies to Teach Factual Information Where Responses Are Greater than Ten. Create pegwords for eleven to nineteen (e.g., eleven = lever, twelve = elf) and for decades (e.g., twenty = *twin*-ty, thirty = thirsty). For example, the fourteenth President of the United States can be remembered by associating Pierce with purse, and "forking" is the pegword for fourteen. Students visualize someone sticking a fork into a purse (Mastropieri et al., 1997).

Use a PEP TALK Strategy to Teach Historical Information. The PEP TALK strategy (**P**erson, **E**vent, and **P**lace; **T**hink PEP, **A**sk questions, **L**ook for answers, **K**eep notes) helps students to focus their reading on finding explicit and implicit information (Katims & Harmon, 2000). First, have the students predict whether they will be reading about a person, event, or place. Then they can focus on answering questions related to that topic. An example of the PEP TALK strategy for learning about the Iceman is provided in Figure 4.11.

Use a Self-Questioning Summarization Strategy. Teach students to identify (a) main ideas in each paragraph and to compare their accuracy with those given in the textbook as textbook subheadings, (b) designate themes for each chapter, and (c) predict test questions (Wong, Wong, Perry, & Sawatsky, 1986).

Attend to the Reading Skills Necessary for Reading Primary Source Documents. Since the handwriting, grammar, and style of historical texts are often different from modern English, students who have reading disabilities may be prevented from accessing such content. You can have these documents transcribed by other students, have them read orally, or otherwise present them in alternate formats that are more accessible.

Explicitly Teach Students Strategies that Help Them Develop Critical Thinking Skills. Learning social studies is not just learning facts. It is also learning how to reason and

---

The Final Hours of the Iceman

Person   _The Iceman_

         Man or Woman? _Man, called Otzi, about 46 years old, 5' 2" and 110 lbs._

         Read and Find:

         What s/he did: _Maybe he got in a fight with other villagers and injured his wrist. He fled to the mountains to get away from his enemies. When he stopped to rest on a mountain, someone shot him with an arrow and pulled the shaft out, leaving the arrow in his body. He probably bled to death._

         Why s/he did it: _Maybe he was more powerful than the other villagers (he was probably rich and he was old for those days) so his enemies fought him for power or for something else._

         When s/he did it: _About 5,300 years ago_.

         Where s/he did it: _Otztal Alps between Austria and Italy_

         Important words: Neolithic, mummified, archaeology, subclavian artery, hemorrhagic shock, glacial.

         Connect: _Mummy exhibit at the museum last month, arrowhead hunting last summer at Grandma's ranch house._

Event   **Read and Find:**
         What happened
         Why it happened
         When it happened
         Where it happened
         Who was involved
         Important words
         Connect

Place   **Read and Find:**
         Where it is
         What it is like
         Why it is special
         Important words
         Connect

Source: National Geographic, July, 2007.

FIGURE 4.11   A Partially Completed Example of the PEP TALK Strategy.

Source: From "Strategic Instruction in Middle School Social Studies: Enhancing Academic and Literacy Outcomes for At-risk Students" By D. S. Katims and J. M. Harmon, _Interventions in School and Clinic, 35_ (5), 2000, 280–289. Reprinted with permission.

evaluate information. Learning is evident when students not only understand information, but when they can also critically evaluate and defend what they have learned. Students with disabilities often lack strategies for developing critical thinking skills and need to be taught how to evaluate knowledge. The PROVE strategy can be used to teach students these skills (Scanlon, 2002). Figure 4.12 outlines the steps of this strategy.

Present the knowledge I will PROVE
(*Write a complete sentence that describes what the student knows about a subject.*)

Reveal information to support my knowledge
(*Provide the rationale or the why statement.*)

Offer evidence to support my knowledge
(*Provide evidence that supports and/or challenges the rationale. The examples explain how the rationale is correct.*)

Verify my knowledge—OPTIONAL STEP
(*If students cannot recall evidence to support the rationale, they should seek out information that will verify and/or challenge their knowledge. Students should make note of sources of information.*)

Express my knowledge in a summary statement
(*Write a complete statement that presents knowledge and accounts for confirming or challenging perspectives.*)

FIGURE 4.12   The PROVE Strategy.

Source: From "PROVE-ing What You Know: Using a Learning Strategy in an Inclusive Class" by D. Scanlon, *TEACHING Exceptional Children, 34* (4), 2002, p. 51. Copyright 2002 by the Council for Exceptional Children. Reprinted with permission.

When teaching students learning strategies, model the strategy, guide students as they practice the strategy, and then provide feedback and correction as the students independently use the strategy.

Allow Opportunities for Whole-Class Responding, Provide Positive Feedback for Correct Answers, and Give Corrective Feedback for Incorrect Answers.   Students can respond to true/false questions by indicating thumbs up/thumbs down. Be sure to let students know when their answers are correct and provide correct information when they are not, either by having other students give correct answers or by prompting the students to obtain the correct answers (Hudson, 1997).

Use Alternative Means to Assess Learning.   Consider assessing learning by having students use multimedia technology (e.g., PowerPoint, HyperStudio), oral presentations, dramatizations, interviews, musical compositions, or group presentations.

Suggestions for Culturally or Linguistically Diverse Students

Little has been published regarding how to instruct culturally or linguistically diverse students with disabilities in the field of social studies. Therefore, social studies teachers should attend to research-based strategies for teaching all students and consider the following suggestions specific to students with mild to moderate disabilities who are culturally or linguistically diverse.

Use a Narrative Framework. Because history is a narrative, or a story of different groups who have encountered a problem, a narrative strategy will provide a framework for understanding historical information. Start narrative learning experiences with an anchor, such as an interesting movie or dramatization to motivate students to discover the problems associated with the narrative (Ferretti et al., 2001).

Teach New Concepts with the Aid of Graphic Organizers in Other Languages. For example, you can teach the causes and effects of the Civil War and use a bilingual organizer to help students understand the concepts that are anchored in their native language (see Figure 4.13).

Nombre (Name) *Beto Fernandez*   Fecha (Date) *March 21*

Causa y Efecto (Cause and Effect)

Evento (Event – *The Civil War*)   Sucede (*Slavery ended, Union was restored, much of the South was destroyed*)

Porque
(Because) *People in the North and South disagreed about slavery.*

Porque
(Because) *People in the North believed that states could not secede from the Union; people in the South believed that states could secede.*

Porque
(Because) *The economy in the North depended on free laborers who received wages, and the economy in the South depended on slave laborers who did not receive wages.*

FIGURE 4.13   The Causes and Effects of the Civil War.

Have Students Argue from Different Perspectives on Issues. For example, to examine the role African Americans played in 1950's mainstream society, have students investigate the issue from different perspectives, allowing them to make their own inquiries, find answers to their questions, and present their findings to the other groups. Be sure to provide students with sufficient explicit instruction on historical reasoning, so as not to promote misunderstandings and misinformation (MacArthur, Ferretti, & Okolo, 2002).

Teach that "Historical Accounts Are Representations of the Past, Constructed by People for Different Purposes" (De La Paz & MacArthur, 2003, p. 151). Discuss how current events or historical accounts would be different if written by different people or for different purposes. For example, after reading a newspaper article about immigration of Mexicans to the United States from the perspective of a white, middle-class U.S. man, have the students reconstruct the article from the perspective of a young Mexican single mother. Note the language differences in each account (e.g., "illegal immigration," "economic necessity") and how some words are value-laden.

Teach Students About the Contributions of Culturally Diverse Individuals.   All students in the classroom can benefit from learning about the contributions of individuals who represent diverse cultures. For example, in lessons you can highlight the accomplishments of Richmond Barthe and Albert L. Cassell (African Americans) in art and architecture, Dennis Chavez and Lauro F Cavazos (Hispanic Americans) in government, Zubin Mehta (Indian Asian American) in music, and Charles A. Eastmond (Ohiyesa–Native American) in literature.

REFERENCES

■ ■ ■ ■ ■ ▬▬▬

Adams, M. A. (1990). *Beginning to read: Thinking and learning about print.* Cambridge, MA: MIT.

American Psychiatric Association. (2000). *Diagnostic and statistical manual of mental disorders* (4th ed., text revision). Washington, DC: Author.

Armbruster, B. B., Lehr, F., & Osborn, J. (2003). *Put reading first: The research building blocks for teaching children to read, kindergarten through grade 3* (2nd ed.). Jessup, MD: National Institute for Literacy.

Ariza, E. N. W. (2006). *Not for ESOL teachers: What every classroom teacher needs to know about the linguistic, culturally, and ethnically diverse student.* Boston: Allyn & Bacon.

Bainbridge, W. L., & Lasley, T. J. (2002). Demographics, diversity, and K–12 accountability: The challenge of closing the achievement gap. *Education and Urban Society, 34,* 422–437.

Bakken, J. P., & Whedon, C. K. (2002). Teaching text structure to improve reading comprehension. *Intervention in School and Clinic, 37,* 229–233.

Barbetta, P. M., & Spears-Bunton, L. A. (2007). Learning to write: Technology for students with disabilities in secondary inclusive classrooms. *English Journal, 96*(4), 86–93.

Beckman, P. (2002). *Strategy instruction.* Arlington, VA: ERIC Clearinghouse on Disabilities and Gifted Education (ERIC Document Reproduction Service No 474302).

Bender, W. N. (2002). *Differentiating instruction for students with learning disabilities.* Thousand Oaks, CA: Corwin.

Bender, W. N., & Larkin, M. J. (2003). *Reading strategies for elementary students with learning disabilities.* Thousand Oaks, CA: Corwin.

Bolt, S. E., & Thurlow, M. L. (2004). Five of the most frequently allowed testing accommodations in state policy: Synthesis of research. *Remedial and Special Education, 25,* 141–152.

Boudah, D. J., Lenz, B. K., Bulgren, J. A., Schumaker, J. B., & Deshler, D. D. (2000). Don't water down! Enhance content through the Unit Organizer Routine. *TEACHING Exceptional Children, 32,* 48–56.

Boyle, J. R. (2001). Enhancing the note-taking skills of students with mild disabilities. *Intervention in School and Clinic, 36,* 221–224.

Boyle, J. R., & Weishaar, M. (2001). The effects of strategic notetaking on recall and comprehension of lecture information for high school students with learning disabilities. *Learning Disabilities Research and Practice, 16,* 133–141.

Bryan, T., & Burstein, K. (2004). Improving homework completion and academic performance: Lessons from special education. *Theory Into Practice, 43,* 213–219.

Bryan, T., & Sullivan-Burstein, K. (1998). Teacher-selected strategies for improving homework completion. *Remedial and Special Education, 19,* 263–275.

Buchan, L., Fish, T., & Prater, M. A. (1996). Teenage Mutant Ninja Turtles counting pizza toppings: Creative writing learning strategy. *TEACHING Exceptional Children, 28,* 40–43.

Bulgren, J. A., Deshler, D. D., & Schumaker, J. B. (1997). Use of a recall enhancement routine and strategies in inclusive secondary classes. *Learning Disabilities Research and Practice, 12,* 198–208.

Burns, M. K. (2004). Empirical analysis of drill ratio research: Refining the instructional level for drill tasks. *Remedial and Special Education, 25,* 167–173.

Burns, M. K. (2005). Using incremental rehearsal to increase fluency of single-digit multiplication facts with children identified as learning disabled in mathematics computation. *Education and Treatment of Children, 28,* 237–249.

139

Carman, R. A., & Adams, W. R. (1984). *Study skills: A student's guide for survival* (2nd ed.). New York: Wiley.

Carter, E. W., Wehby, J., Hughes, C., Johnson, S. M., Plank, D. R., Barton-Arwood, S. M., & Lunsford, L. B. (2005). Preparing adolescents with high-incidence disabilities for high-stakes testing with strategy instruction. *Preventing School Failure, 49*(2), 55–62.

Catts, H. W., & Hogan, T. P. (2003). Language basis of reading disabilities and implications for early identification and remediation. *Reading Psychology, 24,* 223–246.

Cawley, J. F., Foley, T. E., & Miller, J. (2003). Science and students with mild disabilities: Principles of universal design. *Intervention in School and Clinic, 38,* 160–171.

Chamberlain, S. P. (2005). Recognizing and responding to cultural differences in the education of culturally and linguistically diverse learners. *Intervention in School and Clinic, 40,* 195–211.

Chard, D. J., & Osborn, J. (1999). Phonics and word recognition instruction in early reading programs: Guidelines for accessibility. *Learning Disabilities Research and Practice, 14,* 107–117.

Chard, D. J., Vaughn, S., & Tyler, B. (2002). A synthesis of research on effective interventions for building reading fluency with elementary students with learning disabilities. *Journal of Learning Disabilities, 35*(5), 387–406.

Council for Exceptional Children. (2001, Spring). *Current practice alerts: A focus on high-stakes assessment.* Arlington, VA: Author.

De La Paz, S. (2007). Managing cognitive demands for writing: Comparing the effects of instructional components in strategy instruction. *Reading & Writing Quarterly, 23,* 249–266.

De La Paz, S., & Graham, S. (1997). Strategy instruction in planning: Effects on the writing performance and behavior of students with learning disabilities. *Exceptional Children, 63,* 167–181.

De La Paz, S., & MacArthur, C. (2003). Knowing the how and why of history: Expectations for secondary students with and without learning disabilities. *Learning Disability Quarterly, 26*(2), 142–154.

Dobb, F. (2004). *Essential elements of effective science instruction for English learners* (2nd ed.). Los Angeles: California Science Project.

Dyck, N., & Pemberton, J. B. (2002). A model for making decisions about text adaptations. *Intervention in School and Clinic, 38,* 28–35.

Edelen-Smith, P. (1997). How now brown cow: Phoneme awareness activities for collaborative classrooms. *Intervention in School and Clinic, 33,* 103–111.

Elliott, S. N., McKevitt, B. C., & Kettler, R. J. (2002). Testing accommodations research and decision making: The case of "good" scores being highly valued but difficult to achieve for all students. *Measurement and Evaluation in Counseling and Development, 35,* 153–166.

Englert, C. S., Zhao, Y., Dunsmore, K., Collings, N. Y., & Wolbers, K. (2007). Scaffolding the writing of students with disabilities through procedural facilitation: Using an Internet-based technology to improve performance. *Learning Disability Quarterly, 30,* 9–29.

Fahsl, A. J. (2007). Mathematics accommodations for all students. *Intervention in School and Clinic, 4,* 198–203.

Farrell, T. S. C. (2006). *Succeeding with English language learners: A guide for beginning teachers.* Thousand Oaks, CA: Corwin.

Feldman, K., & Denti, L. (2004). High-access instruction: Practical strategies to increase active learning in diverse classrooms. *Focus on Exceptional Children, 37*(7), 3–10.

Ferretti, R. P., Andrews-Weckerly, S., & Lewis, W. E. (2007). Improving the argumentative writing of students with learning disabilities: Descriptive and normative considerations. *Reading & Writing Quarterly, 23,* 267–285.

Ferretti, R., MacArthur, C. D., & Okolo, C. M. (2001). Teaching for historical understanding in inclusive classrooms. *Learning Disability Quarterly, 24,* 59–71.

Finnan, C., Schnepel, K. C., & Anderson, L. W. (2003). Powerful learning environments: The critical link between school and classroom cultures. *Journal of Education for Students Placed At Risk, 8,* 391–418.

Forgrave, K. E. (2002). Assistive technology: Empowering students with learning disabilities. *Assistive Technology, 75,* 122–126.

Fulk, B. J. M, & Montgomery-Grymes, D. J. (1994). Strategies to improve student motivation, *Intervention in School and Clinic, 30*(1). 28–33.

Geary, D. C. (2004). Mathematics and learning disability. *Journal of Learning Disabilities, 37*(1), 4–15.

Gersten, R., Jordan, N. C., & Flojo, J. R. (2005). Early identification and interventions for students with mathematics difficulties. *Journal of Learning Disabilities, 38,* 293–304.

Glazer, S. M. (1996). Getting kids to say more. *Teaching PreK–8, 27*(3), 92–93.

Goodwin, M. W. (1999). Cooperative learning and social skills: What skills to teach and how to teach them. *Intervention in School and Clinic, 35,* 29–33.

Graham, S., & Harris, K. R. (1989). Improving learning disabled students' skills at composing essays: Self-instructional strategy training. *Exceptional Children, 56,* 201–214.

Gut, D. M. (2000). We are social beings: Learning how to learn cooperatively. *TEACHING Exceptional Children, 32*(5), 46–53.

Hadaway, N. L., Vardell, S. M., & Young, T. A. (2004). *What every teacher should know about English language learners.* Boston: Pearson Education.

Harris, K. R., Friedlander, B. D., Saddler, B., Frizelle, R., & Graham, S. (2005). Self-monitoring of attention versus self-monitoring of academic performance: Effects among students with ADHD in the general education classroom. *Journal of Special Education, 39,* 145–156.

Hayes, B. K., & Conway, R. N. (2000). Concept acquisition in children with mild intellectual disability: Factors affecting the abstraction of prototypical information. *Journal of Intellectual & Developmental Disability, 25,* 217–234.

Hill, J. D., & Flynn, K. M. (2006). *Classroom instruction that works with English language learners.* Alexandria, VA: Association for Supervision and Curriculum Development.

Hoover, J. J., & Patton, J. R. (2005). Differentiating curriculum and instruction for English-language learners with special needs. *Intervention in School and Clinic, 40,* 231–235.

Hudson, P. (1996). Using a learning set to increase the test performance of students with learning disabilities in social studies classes. *Learning Disabilities Research and Practice, 11,* 78–85.

Hudson, P. (1997). Using teacher-guided practice to help students with learning disabilities acquire and retain social studies content. *Learning Disability Quarterly, 20*(1), 23–32.

Hughes, C. A., Ruhl, K. L., Schumaker, J. B., & Deshler, D. D. (2002). Effects of instruction in an assignment completion strategy on the homework performance of students with learning disabilities in general education classes. *Learning Disabilities Research, 17*(1), 1–18.

Hughes, C. A., & Schumaker, J. B. (1991). Test-taking strategy instruction for adolescents with learning disabilities. *Exceptionality, 2,* 205–221.

Janney, R. D., & Snell, M. E. (2006). Modifying schoolwork in inclusive classroom. *Theory into Practice, 45*(3), 215–223.

Jarrett, D. (1999). *Mathematics and science instruction for students with learning disabilities: It's just good teaching.* Portland, OR: Northwest Regional Education Laboratory.

Jenkins, J. R., Antil, L. R., Wayne, S. K., & Vadasy, P. F. (2003). How cooperative learning works for special education and remedial students. *Exceptional Children, 69,* 279–292.

Jerger, M. A. (1996). Phoneme awareness and the role of the educator. *Intervention in School and Clinic, 32*(1), 5–13.

Jesness, J. (2004). *Teaching English language learners K–12: A quick-start guide for the new teacher.* Thousand Oaks, CA: Corwin.

Kame'enui, E. J., & Simmons, D. (1999). *Toward successful inclusion of students with disabilities: The architecture of instruction.* Reston, VA: The Council for Exceptional Children.

Katims, D. S., & Harmon, J. M. (2000). Strategic instruction in middle school social studies: Enhancing academic and literacy outcomes for at-risk students. *Interventions in School and Clinic, 35*(5), 280–289.

King-Sears, M. E. (2001). Three steps for gaining access to the general education curriculum for learners with disabilities. *Intervention in School and Clinic, 37*(2) 67–76.

Kozminsky, E., & Kozminsky, L. (2002). The dialogue page: Teacher and student dialogues to improve learning motivation. *Intervention in School and Clinic, 38,* 88–95.

Krug, D., Davis, T. B., & Glover, J. A. (1990). Massed versus distributed repeated reading: A case of forgetting helping recall? *Journal of Educational Psychology, 82,* 366–371.

Lenz, B. K, Ehren, B. J., & Deshler, D. D. (2005). The content literacy continuum: A school reform framework for improving adolescent literacy for all students. *TEACHING Exceptional Children, 37,* 60–63.

Lenz, B. K., & Schumaker, J. B. (1999). *Adapting language arts, social studies, and science materials for the inclusive classroom.* Reston, VA: The Council for Exceptional Children.

Lovett, M. W., Lacerenza, L., Borden, S. L., Frijters, K. A., & Steinbach, M. D. (2000). Components of effective remediation for developmental reading disabilities: Combining phonological and strategy-based instruction to improve outcomes. *Journal of Educational Psychology, 92,* 263–283.

MacArthur, C, Ferretti, R. P., & Okolo, C. M. (2002). On defending controversial viewpoints: Debates of sixth graders about the desirability of early 20th-century American immigration. *Learning Disabilities Research and Practice, 17,* 160–172.

Maheady, L., Harper, G. F., & Mallette, B. (2001). Peer-mediated instruction and interventions and students with mild disabilities. *Remedial and Special Education, 22,* 4–14.

Mastropieri, M. A., Leinart, A., & Scruggs, T. E. (1999). Strategies to increase reading fluency. *Intervention in School and Clinic, 34*(5), 278–283.

Mastropieri, M. A., & Scruggs, T. E. (1998). Enhancing school success with mnemonic strategies. *Intervention in School and Clinic, 33,* 201–208.

Mastropieri, M. A., Scruggs, T. E., & Magnusen, M. (1999). Activities-oriented science instruction for students with disabilities. *Learning Disabilities Quarterly, 22,* 240–249.

Mastropieri, M. A., Scruggs, T. E., & Whedon, C. (1997). Using mnemonic strategies to teach information about U.S. presidents: A classroom-based investigation. *Learning Disability Quarterly, 20*(1), 13–21.

McCay, L. O., & Keyes, D. W. (2002). Developing social competence in the inclusive primary classroom. *Childhood Education, 78,* 70–78.

McCleery, T. A., & Tindal, G. A. (1999). Teaching the scientific method to at-risk students and students with learning disabilities through concept anchoring and explicit instruction. *Remedial and Special Education, 20,* 7–18.

McGinnis, E., & Goldstein, A. P. (1997). *Skillstreaming the elementary school child: New strategies and perspectives for teaching prosocial skills.* Champaign, IL: Research Press.

McLaughlin, B., & McLeod, B. (1996). *Educating all our students: Improving education for children from culturally and linguistically diverse backgrounds.* Final Report of the National Center for Research on Cultural Diversity and Second Language Learning, Volume 1. University of California Santa Cruz.

McNamara, J. K., & Wong, B. (2003). Memory for everyday information in students with learning disabilities. *Journal of Learning Disabilities, 36,* 394–406.

McTighe, J., Seif, E., & Wiggins, G. (2004). You can teach for meaning. *Educational Leadership, 62*(1), 26–30.

Meir, T. (2003). "Why can't she remember that?" The importance of storybook reading in multilingual, multicultural classrooms. *The Reading Teacher, 57,* 243–252.

Miller, S. P., & Hudson, P. J. (2007). Using evidence-based practices to build mathematics competence related to conceptual, procedural, and declarative knowledge. *Learning Disabilities Research & Practice, 22*(1), pp. 47–57.

Mithaug, D. K. (2002). "Yes" means success: Teaching children with multiple disabilities to self-regulate during independent work. *TEACHING Exceptional Children, 35,* 22–27.

Munk, D. D., & Bursuck, W. D. (1998). Report card grading adaptations for students with disabilities: Types and acceptability. *Intervention in School and Clinic, 33,* 306–308.

Murphy, E., Grey, I. M., & Honan, R. (2005). Co-operative learning for students with difficulties in learning: A description of models and guidelines for implementation. *British Journal of Special Education, 32,* 157–164.

National Council for the Social Studies. (1994). *Curriculum standards for social studies.* Washington, DC: Author.

National Dissemination Center for Children with Disabilities. (2002). *Attention deficit/Hyperactivity disorder.* Retrieved January 12, 2007 from http://www.ldonline.org/article/5787?theme=print.

Okolo, C. M., Bahr, C. M., & Gardner, J. E. (1995). Increasing achievement motivation of elementary school students with mild disabilities. *Intervention in School and Clinic, 30,* 279–286.

Padron, Y. N., Waxman, H. C., & Rivera, H. H. (2002). *Educating Hispanic students: Effective instructional practices.* Center for Research on Education, Diversity & Excellence, Practitioner brief #5. Retrieved March 22, 2007 from: http://www.cal.org/crede/pubs/PracBrief5.htm.

Palmer, S. B., & Wehmeyer, M. L. (2003). Promoting self-determination in early elementary school: Teaching self-regulated problem and goal setting skills. *Remedial and Special Education, 24,* 115–126.

Payne, R. K. (2003). *A framework for understanding poverty* (3rd ed.). Highlands, TX: Aha!

Prater, M. A. (1998). Teaching concepts: Procedures for the design and delivery of instruction. *Remedial and Special Education, 14*(5), 51–62.

Prater, M. A. (2007). *Teaching strategies for students with mild to moderate disabilities.* Boston: Allyn & Bacon.

Reyhner, J., & Davison, D. M. (1992). Improving mathematics and science instruction for LEP middle and high school students through language activities. *Proceedings of the Third National Research Symposium on Limited English Proficient Student Issues: Focus on middle and high school issues.* Washington, DC.

Rothstein, L. F. (2000). *Special education law.* (3rd ed.). New York: Addison Wesley Longman.

Salend, S. J. (2005). Report card models that support communications and differentiation of instruction. *TEACHING Exceptional Children, 37,* 28–34.

Salend S. J., & Duhaney, L. M. (2002). Grading students in inclusive settings. *TEACHING Exceptional Children, 34,* 8–15.

Salend, S. J., Elhoweris, H., & van Garderen, D. (2003). Educational interventions for students with ADD. *Intervention in School and Clinic, 38,* 280–288.

Scanlon, D. (2002). PROVE-ing what you know: Using a learning strategy in an inclusive class. *TEACHING Exceptional Children, 34*(4), 48–54.

Schumaker, J. D., & Deschler, D. D. (2003). Can students with LD become competent writers? *Learning Disability Quarterly, 26,* 129–141.

Scruggs, T. E., & Mastropieri, M. A. (1992a). Classroom applications of mnemonic instruction: Acquisition, maintenance, and generalization. *Exceptional Children, 58,* 219–229.

Scruggs, T. E, & Mastropieri, M. A. (1992b). *Teaching test-taking skills: Helping students show what they know.* Cambridge, MA: Brookline.

Semrud-Clikeman, M. (2005). Neuropsychological aspects for evaluating learning disabilities. *Journal of Learning Disabilities, 38,* 563–568.

Sheppard, S. (2001). Tips for teaching: Improving academic success for diverse-language learners. *Preventing School Failure, 45,* 132–135.

Sileo, T. W., & Prater, M. A. (1998). Creating classroom environments that address the linguistic and cultural backgrounds of students with disabilities: An Asian Pacific American perspective. *Remedial and Special Education, 19,* 323–337.

Silva, M., Munk, D. D., & Bursuck, W. D. (2005). Grading adaptations for students with disabilities. *Intervention in School and Clinic, 41,* 87–98.

Silver-Pacuilla, H., & Fleishman, S. (2006). Technology to help struggling students. *Educational Leadership, 75*(3) 84–85.

Steele, M. M. (2004). Teaching science to students with learning problems in the elementary classroom. *Preventing School Failure, 49*(1), 19–21.

Steele, M. M. (2007). Teaching science to students with learning differences. *The Science Teacher, 74,* 24–27.

Stein, M., Kinder, D., Silbert, J., & Carnine, D. (2006). *Designing effective mathematics instruction: A direct instruction approach* (4th ed.). Upper Saddle River, NJ: Prentice Hall.

Stipek, D. (2006). Relationships. *Educational Leadership, 64*(1), 46–49.

Terrill, M. C., Scruggs, T. E., & Mastropieri, M. A. (2004). SAT vocabulary instruction for high school students with learning disabilities. *Intervention in School and Clinic, 39,* 288–294.

Thurlow, M. L., Elliott, J. L., & Ysseldyke, J. E. (2003). *Testing students with disabilities: Practical strategies for complying with district and state requirements* (2nd ed.). Thousand Oaks, CA: Corwin.

Turnbull, R., Turnbull, A., Shank, M., Smith, S., & Leal, D. (2002). *Exceptional lives: Special education in today's schools* (3rd ed.). Upper Saddle River, NJ: Merrill Prentice Hall.

Uberti, H. Z., Scruggs, T. E., & Mastropieri, M. A. (2003). Keywords make the difference! Mnemonic instruction in inclusive classrooms. *Teaching Exceptional Children, 35*(3), 56–61.

U.S. Department of Education, Office of Special Education Programs. (2004). *Teaching children with attention deficit hyperactivity disorder: Instructional strategies and practices.* Retrieved January 12, 2007 from: http://www.ldonline.org/article/8797?theme=print.

van Garderen, D., & Montague, M. (2003). Visual-spatial representation, mathematical problem solving, and students of varying abilities. *Learning Disabilities Research and Practice, 18,* 246–254.

Venn, J. J. (2007). *Assessing students with special needs* (4th ed.). Upper Saddle River, NJ: Pearson.

Watson, S., & Johnston, L. (2007). Assistive technology in the inclusive science classroom: Devices and services can help science students with a wide variety of needs. *The Science Teacher, 74,* (3), 34–38.

Wehrung-Schaffner, L., & Sapona, R. H. (1990). May the FORCE be with you: A test preparation strategy for learning disabled adolescents. *Academic Therapy, 25,* 291–300.

Wong, B. Y. L, Wong, R., Perry, N., & Sawatsky, D. (1986). The efficacy of a self-questioning summarization strategy for use by underachievers and learning disabled adolescents in social studies. *Learning Disability Focus, 2,* 20–35.

Woodward, J., & Noell, J. (1991). Science instruction at the secondary level: Implications for students with learning disabilities. *Journal of Learning Disabilities, 24,* 277–284.

Woodruff, S., Schumaker, J. B., & Deshler, D. D. (2002). *Institute for Academic Access: The effects of an intensive reading intervention on the decoding skills of high school students with reading deficits* (Vol. 15, pp. 2–15). Lawrence: Kansas University.

Xin, Y. P., Jitendra, A. K., & Deatline-Buchman, A. (2005). Effects of mathematical word problem-solving instruction on middle school students with learning problems. *The Journal of Special Education, 39,* 181–192.

Zehler, A. M. (1994). Working with English language learners: Strategies for elementary and middle school teachers. *Office of Bilingual Education and Minority Language Affairs, Program Information Guide Series No. 19.* Washington, D.C.: National Clearinghouse for Bilingual Education.

Zera, D. A., & Lucian, D. G. (2001). Self-organization and learning disabilities: A Theoretical perspective for the interpretation and understanding of dysfunction. *Learning Disability Quarterly, 24,* 107–118.

■ ■ ■ ■ ■

LESSON PLANS

LESSON PLAN FOR TEACHING THE CONCEPT SQUARE

Objective: Given 20 pictures of geometric shapes, students will circle all the squares (8 squares).

Define the concept in clear concise language: Squares have four straight lines. The lines are connected and form "Ls" where they touch. The lines are the same length.

Delivery of Instruction

Define the Concept and Model the Process for Learning the Concept.

1. Say and demonstrate: "Squares have straight lines. The lines on this object are straight."
2. "I count the lines on the object. I count the lines because squares have 4 lines."
3. "This object has four lines."
4. "I check to see if the lines are connected and are the same length. Connected means the lines touch each other. These lines touch and form "Ls" where they touch. They are all the same length."
5. "This is a square. There are four straight lines that touch and form "Ls" where they touch, and the lines are the same length."

Teach Students a Process for Using the Definition of the Square to Discriminate it from Other Geometric Shapes.

1. "Look at the shape. Ask yourself: Are the lines straight or curvy?"
2. "If they are curvy, cross out the shape. It is not a square."
3. "If they are straight and connected count the lines."
4. "If there are three lines, cross out the shape. It is not a square."
5. "If there are four connected lines all the same length, and the lines form "Ls" where they meet, color the object. It is a square."

Guide the Students as they Learn to Apply the Definition and Complete the Process for Discriminating a Square from Other Objects. As you use the same dialogue you used to model the process (substituting "we" for "I"), frequently ask questions to assess learning, and monitor whether the students are correctly following the procedures you are teaching.

Provide Opportunities for Students to Respond Frequently.   Frequently asking questions and prompting the students to complete the process you are teaching will keep them engaged in learning tasks, and will increase the likelihood that they will learn the concept. As you instruct the class to use the process, provide many examples so that the students will have enough practice to learn the process being taught and the concept.

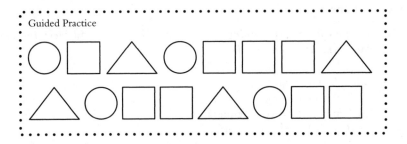

Guided Practice

Monitor Progress and Provide Feedback and Correction.   As the students are working through the practice examples, monitor whether the students are using the process taught to discriminate squares from other objects. Provide feedback and correction when they make errors. For example, if the students count the lines of a triangle and then do not cross out the triangle, restate the process, question them for understanding, and then prompt them to complete the process correctly. "If the number of lines is three, the object is not a square, put an X through the object. What do we do if an object has three lines? Count the lines on this object again. What do you do?"

LESSON PLAN FOR TEACHING A STUDENT
HOW TO SELF-RECORD ON-TASK BEHAVIOR

Objective: When the self-recording beep sounds, student will mark a + for on-task behavior or a 0 for off-task behavior on the self-monitoring sheet 50 of 50 times that the beep sounds.

Delivery of Instruction

Describe the Steps for Self-Recording and Explain Why it Would Help the Student Learn How to Focus Attention in Class.

1. Listen for the recorded beep.
2. Decide if you are on task.
3. Mark a + in the box if you are on task.
4. Mark a 0 in the box if you are off task.

Define On-Task and Off-Task Behavior.

1. On-task behavior is reading, writing, or responding when asked. Pockets are on the chair, feet are on the ground, hands and feet are to self, and the body is facing forward toward the front of the classroom.

2. Off-task behavior is talking with a neighbor, calling out or talking out, playing with things in or on the desk, and doing anything other than reading, writing, or responding as asked. Off task is also standing up or sitting in a position other than facing forward with pockets on the seat and feet on the ground.

Teach the Student How to Self-Record Through Modeling and Guided Practice. Provide Examples of On-Task and Off-Task Behavior.

1. When I record my on-task behavior, I listen for the beep.
2. When I hear the beep, I decide if I am on task. (Explain and demonstrate what on task means.)
3. If I am on task, I mark a + in the first box. (Demonstrate.)
4. If I am not on task, I mark a 0 in the box. (Explain and demonstrate what off task is.)

Monitor Progress and Provide Feedback and Correction.   Provide many opportunities to practice self-recording. Throughout instruction and guided practice, ask questions to ensure student understanding. Monitor how the student rates his or her behavior and provide feedback and correct errors when needed. If necessary, re-teach steps. Move to independent practice only when the student has demonstrated he or she can accurately record his or her behavior.

Provide Independent Practice.

1. Say, "You are now ready to record your behavior."
2. Play the *beep tape* during one period of instruction and have the student record his or her on/off-task behavior each time the beep sounds.
3. Provide feedback as the student self-records.
4. Record data from the student's record-keeping form.

Review.   Periodically review the definitions of on-task and off-task behavior and the procedures for self-recording.

LESSON PLAN FOR TEACHING A STRATEGY

Making Connections

Objective: When given a list of five new social studies or science vocabulary words, students will write the new words, write what they already know about the words, write definitions of the words, and provide an example or illustration of each definition.

Delivery of Instruction

Describe the Steps for Connecting New Learning with Prior Knowledge and Explain Why Making Connections Facilitates Learning.

1. Write the new word.
2. Think of what you already know about the word.
3. Look up the definition of the word and explain how the definition is the same or different from what you thought.
4. Provide an example or illustration of the new term or concept.

Teach the Student the Steps of Making Associations Through Modeling and Guided Practice.

1. When I make connections, the first thing I do is I write the new vocabulary word in the first column of my table. (See the table below for an instructional example.)
2. Then, I think about what I already know about the word and write it in the second column of the table.

NEW WORD	WHAT I KNOW	DICTIONARY DEFINITION	EXAMPLE
metamorphosis	Metamorphosis is when something changes and becomes different. Transformers can change shape.	A marked or developmental change in the form or structure of an animal (as a butterfly or a frog) occurring subsequent to birth or hatching. The structure of the animal changes after the animal is born. With living things, the change cannot be reversed.	A butterfly starts out as a caterpillar and changes into a butterfly.

3. In the third column of the table, I write a definition of the word. If the definition is different from what I thought the term meant, I explain how my thinking was different.
4. In the fourth column, I provide an example or illustration of the new word.

Monitor Progress and Provide Feedback and Correction.   Provide many opportunities for students to practice making connections. Throughout instruction and guided practice, ask questions to ensure student understanding. Monitor their work and provide feedback and correct errors when needed. If necessary, re-teach steps. Move to independent practice only when students have demonstrated they can implement the strategy with very little assistance.

Provide Independent Practice.

1. Say, "You are now ready to make connections on your own."
2. Give students a list of the new vocabulary terms (e.g., fragmentation, canopy, permafrost) and instruct them to complete the table on their own.
3. Provide feedback on their application of the procedure.

Review.   Periodically review how to make connections and continue to provide opportunities for students to practice the skill.

LESSON PLAN FOR TEACHING TEST-TAKING STRATEGIES

Objective: When given five sample tests, the student will write *SCORER* at the top of each test and check off each letter after following through with the appropriate steps of the mnemonic strategy.

Delivery of Instruction

Describe the SCORER Procedures and Explain Why it Would Help Students to Learn and Apply the Procedures.

1. Say, "How would you like to score higher on your subject matter tests? I will teach you a strategy that will help you do better on tests."
2. Say and write, "The strategy is called SCORER. It is easy to remember because if you know the content on which you are being tested and you use SCORER, you will score better on tests. The first thing you do is write SCORER at the top of your page."

Teach the SCORER Procedure Through Modeling and Guided Practice.

1. Say and write, "The word SCORER starts with S. S stands for schedule time. What does S stand for? One thing that can happen when you take a test is running out of time. So it is important for you to know how much time you have to take the test and how long the test is. Then you can decide how much time you can spend on each section. Once you have done that you can check off the S."

2. Using a sample test, demonstrate writing SCORER at the top. Verbalize that you remember S stands for schedule time. Then show students how you would schedule your time. For example, knowing you have 45 minutes to complete the test, but 30 questions, you decide to spend about 1 minute on each question which will give you time at the end to go back and review. Once you have completed the step, verbalize that you remember you are supposed to check off the S when you have completed the step. Check the S.

3. Distribute sample tests to students. Guide them through writing SCORER at the top of the test and implementing scheduling their time. Use questions such as, "What are you supposed to do first?" "Then what do you do?" Provide ample opportunities to practice.

4. Repeat the above steps for the remaining letters:
    a. **C**lue words, look for
    b. **O**mit difficult questions (if there is no penalty for skipping questions)
    c. **R**ead carefully
    d. **E**stimate answers
    e. **R**eview your work

Monitor Progress and Provide Feedback and Correction.   Provide many opportunities to practice. Throughout instruction and guided practice, ask questions to ensure student understanding. Monitor their work and provide feedback and correct errors when needed. If necessary, re-teach steps. Move to independent practice only when students have demonstrated they can implement the strategy with very little assistance.

Provide Independent Practice.

1. Say, "You are now ready to practice the SCORER procedure on your own."
2. Have students take timed practice tests and apply the SCORER procedure.
3. Provide feedback on their application of the SCORER procedure.

Review.   Periodically review the SCORER procedure, particularly before they take a high-stakes test or a classroom-based test that will impact their grade.

■ ■ ■ ■ ■

CONCEPT ANCHORING TABLE

KNOWN INFORMATION	KNOWN CONCEPT: LEMONADE BUSINESS		NEW CONCEPT: COMMENSALISM
Lemonade sugar, boy, space, stand, neighbor, cups	Characteristics of Known Concept ⟶	Characteristics Shared	Characteristics of New concept ⟵
	Boy and a neighbor	2 living things (A & B)	2 organisms (barnacles & gray whales)
	Neighbor gives boy lawn space for lemonade stand	A is helped	One (barnacle) is helped by other (gray whale)
	Neighbor gets nothing/loses nothing	B is not helped/not harmed	Helper (gray whale) gets nothing/loses nothing

Summary Statement: Commensalism is a relationship between two living things in which Organism A is helped and Organism B is not helped or harmed.

Source: From *Adapting Language Arts, Social Studies, and Science Materials for the Inclusive Classroom* by K. Lenz, and K. Schumaker. Reston, VA: Council for Exceptional Children. Copyright 1999 by the Council for Exceptional Children. Reprinted with permission.

UNIT ORGANIZER

The "Big Picture" (The Roots and Consequences of Civil Unrest)

LAST UNIT EXPERIENCES GROWTH OF THE NATION	CURRENT UNIT THE CAUSES OF THE CIVIL WAR	NEXT UNIT THE CIVIL WAR

Schedule of assignments

1/22 Cooperative Groups, pp. 220–228.

1/28 Quiz

1/30 Cooperative Groups, pp. 230–245.

2/4 Review for Test

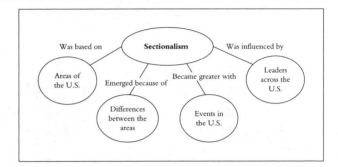

Unit Self-Test Questions

1. What was sectionalism as it existed in the U.S. of 1860?
2. How did the differences in the sections of the U.S. in 1860 contribute to the start of the Civil War?
3. What examples of sectionalism exist in the world today?

Unit Relationship

descriptive

compare/contrast

cause/effect

Unit Organizer—Second Page

Expanded Unit Map

The Causes of the Civil War

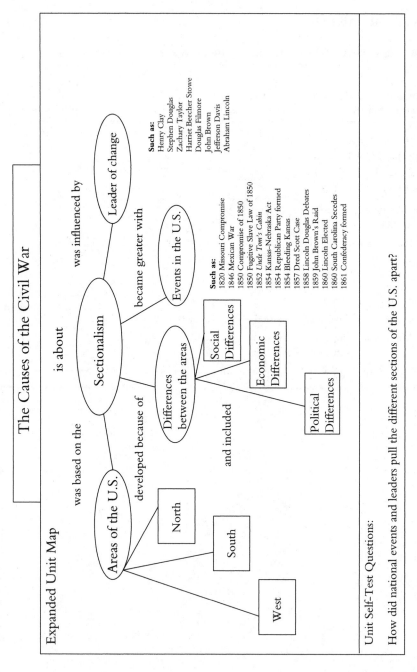

Unit Self-Test Questions:

How did national events and leaders pull the different sections of the U.S. apart?

■ ■ ■ ■ ■